Let your geek shine.

Meet Pete Lewis, lead vocalist for the band
Storytyme. Pete recently created the RS1000,
a new personal monitor system for performing
musicians. It was SparkFun's tutorials, products
and PCB service that enabled him to take his idea
to market in less than a year.

The tools are out there. Find the resources you
need to let your geek shine too.

Sharing Ingenuity
WWW.SPARKFUN.COM

Make:
Volume 15
technology on your time®

ON THE COVER: The Guitar Zeros rock to the fullest, DIY style, in Brooklyn, N.Y. Photographed by Elena Dorfman and styled by Sam Murphy. Thanks to Julian Honoré for the awesome lighting bolt.

Columns

BEAM ME UP:
Stephen Hobley strums a celestial synth solo on his laser harp.

+ makezine.com
Visit for story updates and extras, Weekend Project videos, podcasts, forums, the Maker Shed, and the award-winning MAKE blog!

Vol. 15, Aug., 2008. MAKE (ISSN 1556-2336) is published quarterly by O'Reilly Media, Inc. in the months of March, May, August, and November. O'Reilly Media is located at 1005 Gravenstein Hwy. North, Sebastopol, CA 95472, (707) 827-7000. SUBSCRIPTIONS: Send all subscription requests to MAKE, P.O. Box 17046, North Hollywood, CA 91615-9588 or subscribe online at makezine.com/offer or via phone at (866) 289-8847 (U.S. and Canada); all other countries call (818) 487-2037. Subscriptions are available for $34.95 for 1 year (4 quarterly issues) in the United States; in Canada: $39.95 USD; all other countries: $49.95 USD. Periodicals Postage Paid at Sebastopol, CA, and at additional mailing offices. POSTMASTER: Send address changes to MAKE, P.O. Box 17046, North Hollywood, CA 91615-9588. Canada Post Publications Mail Agreement Number 41129568. CANADA POSTMASTER: Send address changes to: O'Reilly Media, PO Box 456, Niagara Falls, ON L2E 6V2

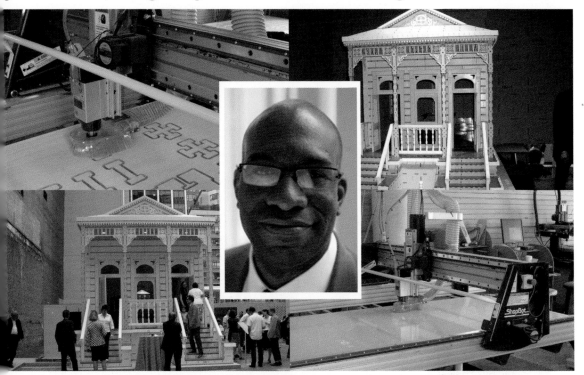

Make: Projects

Compressed Air Rocket

Blow your friends away as you send this 25-cent rocket hundreds of feet in the air. By Rick Schertle

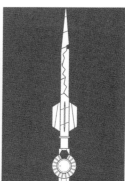

Vortex Cannons

Choose between 3 cannons that can throw "chunks of air" across a room. By Edwin Wise

The Amazing Seebeck Generator

This simple energy-recycling dynamo turns heat from a candle into usable electricity. By Andrew Lewis

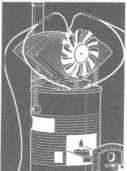

BUILD NOTES

Make:

The iConveyor

Use microchipped wooden tiles to launch your favorite websites and applications.
By John Edgar Park

Project: Wireless Watchdog	
Created by: Dave Kuhl	

Parts:

 + + + + +

Notes:

When I would get home from work, I kept noticing my fridge door was open. I couldn't figure out what was going on. So I set up a webcam in the house. This way, I could check on things from anywhere using my wireless phone's Internet browser. Turned out, it was an inside job. For ideas and other creations from RadioShack, check out rsinventionslab.com.

Make:
technology on your time®

Volume 15

READ ME: Always check the URL associated with a project before you get started. There may be important updates or corrections.

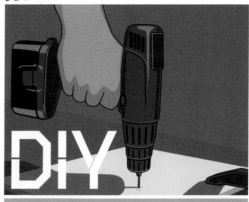

Maker

HELL BENT:
Tim Kaiser bends circuits and minds with his homemade instruments.

[**GEEKED AT BIRTH.**]

LEARN:

DIGITAL ANIMATION	**GAME PROGRAMMING**
DIGITAL ART AND DESIGN	NETWORK SECURITY
DIGITAL VIDEO	NETWORK ENGINEERING
GAME DESIGN	SOFTWARE ENGINEERING
ARTIFICIAL LIFE PROGRAMMING	WEB ARCHITECHTURE
COMPUTER FORENSICS	ROBOTICS & EMBEDDED SYSTEMS

You can talk the talk. Can you walk the walk? Here's a chance to prove it. Please geek responsibly. **www.uat.edu** > 877.UAT.GEEK
877.828.4335

Make:
technology on your time™

EDITOR AND PUBLISHER
Dale Dougherty
dale@oreilly.com

EDITOR-IN-CHIEF
Mark Frauenfelder
markf@oreilly.com

CREATIVE DIRECTOR
Daniel Carter
dcarter@oreilly.com

MANAGING EDITOR
Shawn Connally
shawn@oreilly.com

DESIGNERS
Katie Wilson
Alison Kendall

ASSOCIATE MANAGING EDITOR
Goli Mohammadi

PRODUCTION DESIGNER
Gerry Arrington

SENIOR EDITOR
Phillip Torrone
pt@makezine.com

PHOTO EDITOR
Sam Murphy
smurphy@oreilly.com

PROJECTS EDITOR
Paul Spinrad
pspinrad@makezine.com

ONLINE MANAGER
Tatia Wieland-Garcia

STAFF EDITOR
Arwen O'Reilly Griffith

ASSOCIATE PUBLISHER
Dan Woods
dan@oreilly.com

COPY CHIEF
Keith Hammond

CIRCULATION DIRECTOR
Heather Harmon

EDITOR AT LARGE
David Pescovitz

ACCOUNT MANAGER
Katie Dougherty

MARKETING & EVENT MANAGER
Rob Bullington

MAKE TECHNICAL ADVISORY BOARD
Evil Mad Scientist Laboratories, Limor Fried, Joe Grand, Saul Griffith, William Gurstelle, Bunnie Huang, Tom Igoe, Mister Jalopy, Steve Lodefink, Erica Sadun

PUBLISHED BY O'REILLY MEDIA, INC.
Tim O'Reilly, CEO
Laura Baldwin, COO

Visit us online at makezine.com
Comments may be sent to editor@makezine.com

For advertising inquiries, contact:
Katie Dougherty, 707-827-7272, katie@oreilly.com

For event inquiries, contact:
Sherry Huss, 707-827-7074, sherry@oreilly.com

Customer Service cs@readerservices.makezine.com
Manage your account online, including change of address at:
makezine.com/account
866-289-8847 toll-free in U.S. and Canada
818-487-2037, 5 a.m.–5 p.m., PST

EVEN GREENER: NEW SOY INK!
MAKE is printed on acid-free, recycled paper containing 30% post-consumer waste, with soy-based inks containing 22%–26% renewable raw materials. Subscriber copies of MAKE, Volume 15, were shipped in recyclable plastic bags.

PLEASE NOTE: Technology, the laws, and limitations imposed by manufacturers and content owners are constantly changing. Thus, some of the projects described may not work, may be inconsistent with current laws or user agreements, or may damage or adversely affect some equipment. Your safety is your own responsibility, including proper use of equipment and safety gear, and determining whether you have adequate skill and experience. Power tools, electricity, and other resources used for these projects are dangerous, unless used properly and with adequate precautions, including safety gear. Some illustrative photos do not depict safety precautions or equipment, in order to show the project steps more clearly. These projects are not intended for use by children.
Use of the instructions and suggestions in MAKE is at your own risk. O'Reilly Media, Inc., disclaims all responsibility for any resulting damage, injury, or expense. It is your responsibility to make sure that your activities comply with applicable laws, including copyright.

Contributing Editors: Gareth Branwyn, William Gurstelle, Mister Jalopy, Brian Jepson, Charles Platt

Contributing Artists: Scott Beale, Matt Blum, Michael Thad Carter, Damien Correll, Elena Dorfman, Steve Double, Jason Forman, Dan Formosa, Paul Freedman, Kyle George, Gabriela Hasbun, Julian Honoré, Alison Kendall, Timmy Kucynda, Tim Lillis, Cody Pickens, Skip Russell, Damien Scogin, Edy Shuetz, Jen Siska, Tina Williams

Contributing Writers: Tim Anderson, Thomas J. Arey, Nate Bell, Jay Burlage, Collin Cunningham, Doug Desrochers, Cory Doctorow, Nick Dragotta, George Dyson, Owen Grace, Saul Griffith, Karen K. Hansen, George W. Hart, Stephen Hobley, Frank Joy, Jay Laney, Ken Lange, Andrew Lewis, Brian McNamara, Terrie Miller, Jim Moir, Buzz Moran, Justin Morris, Mose O'Griffin, Ryan O'Horo, Luigi Oldani, Meara O'Reilly, John Edgar Park, Tom Parker, Michael H. Pryor, Publius, James Robertson, Tom Rodgers, Don Reisinger, Hugh Young Rienhoff Jr., Erica Sadun, Rick Schertle, Brian Schmierer, Carol Scott, Donald E. Simanek, Eric Smillie, Bruce Sterling, Bruce Stewart, Alex Sugg, Christopher Thompson, Nat Torkington, Michael Una, Megan Mansell Williams, Edwin Wise, Thomas Zimmerman, Lee David Zlotoff

Bloggers: Jonah Brucker-Cohen, Collin Cunningham, Kip Kedersha, Becky Stern, Marc de Vinck

Interns: Luke Dahlin (engr.), Matthew Dalton (engr.), Adrienne Foreman (web), Arseny Lebedev (web), Kris Magri (engr.), Ed Troxell (edit.)

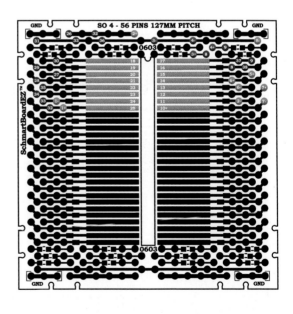

Contributors

Rick Schertle (*Air Rocket*) has taught middle school for the last 15 years in San Jose, where he lives with his wife and young son and daughter. As a kid, he and his dad tried many things and became experts at none, but had a lot of fun along the way. As an adult, his projects have become bigger, like his latest, converting an old Mercedes to run on veggie oil. His family inspires his projects, and together they enjoy their backyard chickens, world travel, and camping. With a love of nature and simple living, Rick often wonders whether modern technology enriches or unnecessarily complicates our lives.

When **Katie Dougherty** (MAKE account manager) isn't busy "convincing companies to get behind the DIY movement," she's riding horses, traveling, spending time outdoors, or reading. She competes with her horse Willoughby, who "takes magic naps in his stall where he lays out like a dog and twitches and snores in his sleep — not normal for a horse!" Her passion for horses is well known at the office, but she's also interested in sustainability and "knowing where my food comes from." She's famous for her mojitos and horse cookies, but not necessarily in that order.

Karen Hansen (Tim Kaiser profile) is a Minnesota farm girl turned "urban junkie." Blame it on dropping out of school at 18 to work in Paris and Berlin. Now an allegedly grown-up clarinetist and writer, Karen has studied in London and worked on assignment in Norway and Denmark. Her favorite jobs out of classical mode have been orchestra gigs with the Merce Cunningham Dance Company in a granite quarry and with the Moody Blues engulfed in marijuana smoke, and interviews with musicians at the Bent Festival. Karen runs around the lakes in Minneapolis, where she lives with LOHL Bill and six clarinets.

Elena Dorfman (cover photographer) currently resides in New York, overlooking the busy waterway of the Hudson River. A photographer and filmmaker, she just completed a five-minute film on horse racing. This is her second shoot for MAKE, and she has enjoyed both experiences immensely. You can see her work at elenadorfman.com.

Doug Desrochers (*Wind Tunnel*) has been voiding warranties, often to his parents' dismay, since early childhood. One of his passions is airplanes: he started flying at age 16, graduated and instructed at the U.S. Naval Test Pilot School, and currently flies tests for ASEC, Inc. His very patient wife humors him, and his two kids are alternately amused and embarrassed by his maker antics, which include model rockets, basic machines, breadboarding electronics, and general goofiness. He has just about every type of tool in the book, after moving into a "money pit" five years ago and rebuilding the house room by room.

"A physician at heart," **Hugh Young Rienhoff Jr.** (*My Daughter's DNA*) lives on the San Francisco Peninsula with his many-talented wife, three children, and "a variable number of rabbits." When he's not developing a drug to help children with beta thalassemia to manage their iron overload from blood transfusions, he makes waffles and builds radios with equal excitement. How does he feel about genetics? "The field is lost and needs to return to its roots of patient orientation. Too many people have genetic conditions that can be understood if we would only use the technology for their benefit." But don't worry, he says. "It will happen."

Sharing the Adventure

In my conversations with makers, we often talk about our favorite books. Frequently it's an out-of-print book, such as *How to Make and Fly Paper Airplanes* by retired Navy Capt. Ralph S. Barnaby, published in 1968. Saul Griffith told me about Barnaby recently and said that his was the very best book on aerodynamics. Saul's office, incidentally, is located in the control tower overlooking a defunct Navy airbase, where he is building high-tech kites.

At O'Reilly's FOO Camp this year, I went to a session titled "Beekeeping, Old Houses, and the Art of Observation." I started keeping two hives of bees this spring. Brian Fitzpatrick, an engineer with Google in Chicago, started the session by introducing his favorite book: *The Art and Adventure of Beekeeping* by Ormond and Harry Aebi. (Ormond, the humble son of a beekeeper, credited his father as co-author.)

Brian is not a beekeeper, but he owns an old house that needs work. This book spoke to him about patience and the power of observation. Are we too quick to think we understand something? If it's a problem we see, we jump in and try to fix it, but maybe we create more problems. That's true for repairing old houses as well as writing software. We don't observe closely for very long.

However, that's exactly what Ormond Aebi did with his bees. Brian lent me a copy of the 1975 book, which is currently out of print. Good writing of this kind doesn't seem to age. Aebi's book is a fine example and belongs to a genre of instructional manual that contains a deeply personal story. We get to see bees the way Aebi sees bees, and perhaps even see him the way bees do. He is devoted to understanding their language. A beekeeper "cannot readily change his bees," he says. "It is he who must make the required adjustments."

Aebi's observations and his detailed procedures are invaluable to someone like me who's trying to learn how to work comfortably with bees, and who doesn't have nearly enough time to sit with his bees as Aebi did. He says you can learn a lot about what bees are doing to by getting up at night and putting your ear up against the hive to listen.

I was mesmerized by Aebi's story of how he captured a swarm high up in a tree. On an extension ladder, with his sleeves rolled up to his shoulder, our hero grabs the branch from which the swarm hangs with one hand, and with the other begins to saw. The branch dips down.

He writes: "This will cause a mass of bees to be dislodged from the lower end of the swarm and they will fall almost to the ground before taking wing. Up they will come with a tremendous buzzing — but they mean no harm." I stop reading and contemplate the beautiful image of bees tumbling down and then rising.

> Our hero grabs the branch from which the swarm of bees hangs with one hand, and with the other begins to saw.

Aebi continues: "This gets to be hard work, for one is standing with one foot on a ladder rung and the other leg hooked over the next higher rung to keep in balance while sawing. I lay aside (sometimes have to drop) the saw as soon as possible and grasp the sawed-off branch with both hands."

So our hero stands atop a tall ladder trying to steady this swarm of bees before he can descend. "The end of the limb with the bees is now hanging lower than my hands. Bees always want to climb upward so in a few minutes they start to cross the few inches of bark between my hands and the swarm. Moments later they begin to cross my bare fingers and climb my bare arms. This is a bit scary."

And I'm thinking, "Yeah."

Aebi waits patiently for the bees to re-cluster, descends the ladder very slowly, and puts the swarm into a waiting hive box without ever being stung. I was awfully glad he shared that adventure, along with so much of his hard-won knowledge. I'm also glad Brian shared a favorite book with me.

Dale Dougherty is the editor and publisher of MAKE and CRAFT magazines.

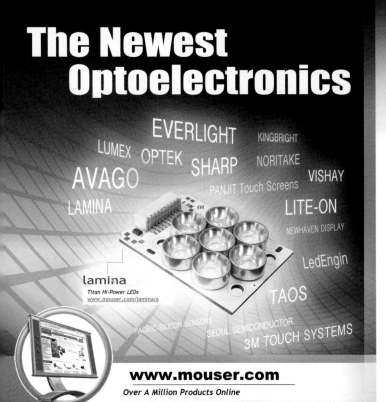

Gander Sauce for Hollywood

When someone proposes a Draconian punishment, it's a sure bet he imagines that it will apply only to *other people* — so an easy way to point out that a punishment goes over the top is to ask the proposer whether he'd be willing to be subjected to it. If it's sauce for the goose, it ought to be sauce for the gander, too.

The entertainment industry is obsessed with kicking people off the internet. When the first round of internet lawmaking was underway in 1995 and 1996, none of Hollywood's "visionaries" imagined that our personal computers would have direct, always-on internet connections and be able to run server software, so the law about copyright infringement online focuses entirely on what to do about pirated works on web servers.

These rules, called "notice and takedown," create a dangerously simple process whereby anyone can contact any internet service provider (ISP) and swear that some web page infringes his copyright. The ISP must remove the material right away, or face prosecution as a party to the infringement.

Not only does this open the way for any petty censor who wants to take down criticism but it's totally useless against peer-to-peer (P2P) file sharing. With P2P, the ISP has no files to take down since the files are all hosted on the users' computers.

Hence the obsession with kicking users off the internet. The idea is that after receiving a couple of unsubstantiated accusations of copyright infringement, your ISP would have a duty to cut off your internet connection.

Now, think for a moment about the proportionality of this response. The internet isn't just a wire that delivers the odd MP3 file. It delivers *everything* — it is a single wire that carries freedom of speech, freedom of the press, and freedom of assembly. It's the connection to your family, to your friends, your doctor, your government, your employer, and your school. It's the largest library ever assembled.

Even if you stipulate that taking someone's music without permission is wrong, is it *that* wrong? Stealing cars is wrong, but we don't take away car thieves' library cards. Even murderers get to go to correspondence school while they do time.

> The entertainment industry is obsessed with kicking people off the internet.

All right, so the entertainment industry believes that taking its reruns and singles is the worst crime in the world. Shouldn't they at least have to prove that someone has done wrong before that person loses access to the net? They say no. They say infringement is so widespread that they couldn't possibly find the time to go to a judge and show evidence every time someone violates copyright law. They need — and deserve — to be judge, jury, and executioner. Trust them, they won't abuse this power. They promise.

Let's hope that they're more careful about who gets to use the internet than they are about who loses their life savings in copyright lawsuits. Viacom sent 100,000 takedown notices to YouTube last year, serving notice on anything that contained the name of any Viacom property. The RIAA has sued dead people and people who don't own computers.

If this is all so reasonable, let's try a little gander sauce: let's have a three-strikes rule for people who send takedown and termination notices. If you send three takedown notices for material that isn't yours, all your web pages get taken off the internet. If you send three termination notices to people who aren't file-sharing infringing material, your entire company is removed from the internet forever.

That's right: if Fox News sends three bad takedowns to YouTube, we take the whole Fox News website offline, forever. If Warner Music wrongfully accuses three internet users of sharing their music on P2P, we go to the Warner Music offices in Los Angeles, London, New York, and all over the world with bolt cutters and sever their connection to the internet, permanently. Sounds fair to me!

Cory Doctorow lives in London, writes science fiction novels, co-edits Boing Boing, and fights for digital freedom.

Makers tell their tales of mad boating experiments and childhood hijinks.

I love MAKE, Volume 12, and I plan on getting many more issues in the future. I'm writing because I think that the article "Building the Barrage Garage" by William Gurstelle, page 32, left out some key elements. I would like to think of myself as a jack of all trades, master of none when it comes to home construction. I know enough to do an addition or workshop area, but there were things in the article I felt needed to be explained, such as the half cinder block, half wood frame construction: why that choice? And while the use of a concrete floor in a workshop is understood by most craftspeople, it may be necessary to explain that choice to some.

When I saw the article I was super excited, but as I read it I felt rushed through it. I understand that most of this phase was contracted out, but the construction aspect is something that many people would like to take on as a DIY project. The details of why choices were made; implementing them; and dealing with permits, ordinances, and building codes all make for an article that could have spanned several more pages.

I look forward to the future installments of this article to see how the writer designs the workspace, and what type of workstations make the cut.

Thank you, again, for a great magazine. Now if only I could move out of this apartment and into a place with a garage for all my tools.

—*Matthew Mahoney*
Harrisburg, Pa.

I'm a huge fan of Halloween and I love the features you've done on the dark holiday.

I was hoping you could tell me who the artist was who produced this terrific image (among others) for your site. I *love* them. Really terrific works.

—*John Altomari*
Pompton Lakes, N.J.

Editor's Note: The graphic artist Seth was the genius behind that image. He's one of the top graphic novelists around these days and we were thrilled to have him illustrate our special issue. Luckily, we still have a few copies available at makezine.com/go/diyhalloween.

I have an expression: "Look what happened while I was sleeping!" I dropped your mag into my 14-year-old son's lap. Yesterday he was back in the woodshop talking about building stuff! Three cheers. Not only will I subscribe, but also I will give it away.

I grew up in the "make it yourself" house. My dad worked at Greibach Instruments where they hand-made precision electric meters. I played with relays, push buttons, and microswitches. This was 1960. We called them "gadget boards" and used 6V transformers to power the lights and relays. For the most part society has lost this hands-on capability, but the "makers" are clearly reviving it.

By the way, are you familiar with the encyclopedia, circa 1950s, by *Popular Mechanics*? I bought a set last year for 15 bucks on eBay.

—*Peter A. Blacksberg*
Wayne, N.J.

Illustration by Seth

Photograph by Ryan O'Horo

✉ I had to share this project with you, it's so amusing. It looks like I just escaped from Cuba in it.

I saw plans for this 1940s-era micro-boat while Googling (simplicityboats.com/corky.html), and thought it would be a hoot to scale it up from a kid-sized contraption to an adult-sized sailer, length about 50". I sailed mine last week.

It can be built and painted in one day, sailed the next. Cost: about $25 for the tube, plus another $30 in materials for the wood, brass screws, and a quart of porch paint to seal it. The sail is made from a simple plastic tarp sewn onto the spars using weed-whacker monofilament; the mast was a closet pole from Wal-Mart.

The entire thing fits in a car trunk when deflated and rolled up. The wood part is basically just a plank under the waterline that connects the "bow" (holding up the detachable mast) to the "stern" with its rudder, and the entire assembly hangs suspended from the inner tube by web belts.

I modified the original design by scaling up the proportions for the larger tube and adding a detachable keel on the bottom which lets you sail closer to the wind for tacking, and not just straight downwind. My simplified rudder is attached with brass door hinges that have removable pins.

As seen in the photo, you actually ride it sideways,

feet and head dangling out on either side. It would be very hard to tip over, and all the parts float, no matter what happens to the inner tube, which is fairly rugged. The more wind, the better it works. For next season I'm working out how to make a lighter, nimbler, more compact traveling version using telescoping PVC pipe.

Enjoy!

—Mark Suszko
Springfield, Ill.

P.S. Keep up the good work, and I'd like to see more boating articles in future issues.

✉ I love your magazine, I really do. I read it cover to cover and enjoy 99.9% of every issue. But Volume 14's article on "Mall Living" [page 34] was out of line. Michael Townsend and Adriana Yoto broke the law, yet the interview questions were worded in a way that, in my opinion, almost condones their actions.

Ten pages earlier is an article that inspires us to try and find ways to make our world better ("The Power of Things") by understanding our power consumption and then reducing it. I guess these two found a way — too bad it was completely unethical. The article uses the word *artist* to describe Townsend, but let's be honest — the word should be changed to *criminal*.

—Jim Kelly
Atlanta, Ga.

MAKE AMENDS

In MAKE, Volume 13, page 137, the "Smart Structure" materials list incorrectly gave capacitor values in microfarads. It should have called for nanofarad values.

In MAKE, Volume 12, page 112, a schematic diagram is missing an arrow to indicate which direction to align diode D1. The arrow should point to the right, just like diode D2.

Photography courtesy of Krištof Kintera

Shock and Awesome

Krištof Kintera likes to make people nervous. He installs spinning circular saws in gallery floors, and rigs the plug at the end of an electric cord to release 50,000 volts in short bursts.

Artworks that, just like your neighbor's home-made flamethrower, scream "Stay away, don't touch!" and then, after the initial jolt of fear, turn out to be super fun.

The Czech artist's latest cringe-inducing master-piece, *Do it yourself (after Brancusi)*, is a 23-foot stack of cement bags that tilts dangerously to one side, looming over spectators.

"Everybody has the intense feeling that this tall tower is about to fall over," Kintera says cheerfully. "It could fall, but it won't," he adds, "and I won't tell you how it's done." Those looking for reassurance should visit his website for the list of building materials. Here's a hint: styrofoam.

Even his non-threatening works are subtly dis-turbing. *Something electric*, a coconut that bobbles absurdly at the end of an extension cord, is hardly dangerous, except perhaps to its creator, who built it out of an eccentric motor and a BASIC Stamp microcontroller.

"I blew up many, many models while building it," Kintera confesses. What's the point of such a senseless appliance? He responds with a typical artist's riddle: "I like to use ready-made materials the way other sculptors work with clay. They're the clay of everyday life."

Despite all his provocative intentions, however, Kintera is still a handyman at heart. "For me, when a piece is finished, it loses its sense of tension and adventure," he says. "You can only experience that thrill when you make it yourself." Or when daring your buddy to touch the sparking end of that live wire.

—*Eric Smillie*

≫ **Krištof Kintera Creations:** kristofkintera.com

Form and Functions

David Jones really liked his old Casio CFX-400 scientific calculator watch. As a professional electronics design engineer, he appreciated the greater functionality it had over other calculator watches, which typically support only the four basic functions. He was saddened when his 20-year-old Casio finally bit the dust, so when he looked around and realized there was no one making scientific calculator watches anymore, he decided to make his own.

He calls it the μWatch ("MicroWatch"). His goals were to make a scientific calculator watch that was good-looking and practical, and could be assembled from off-the-shelf parts.

"I could have designed a custom case for it, and used custom parts to get the size down and make it look like a store-bought watch, but there was no fun in that! Using off-the-shelf parts was a real challenge and in the end was the most satisfying aspect of the project," Jones recalls.

A resident of Sydney, Jones has been publishing projects in Australian electronics magazines since

he was 15. Besides his μWatch, he's designed and built his own solar air heater called the Solar Sponge, and written an interactive exercise program that runs on iPods and other MP3 players. He also likes to get involved with serious home renovation projects.

Jones has released his μWatch source code under the GPL to encourage third-party development, and he sells kits for those interested in building one. He includes a complete schematic and detailed photos on his website.

And the μWatch isn't limited to being just a scientific calculator. Its programming port, universal I/O port, and optional infrared remote interface let you connect it to almost anything. "With the two-line LCD, full keypad, and 16-bit microprocessor, it's really a powerful general-purpose computing and control platform," Jones points out.

If you want a μWatch that controls your TV, plays games, or commands other user-designed devices, just add some software. —*Bruce Stewart*

>> **Build Your Own:** calcwatch.com

Photograph by David Olsen

Interstellar Visions

Down a lonely stretch of Sonoran desert highway south of Tucson, Ariz., lies the washboarded pull-off for Interstellar Light Applications. Visitors don't have to wait for the dust to settle to lay eyes on ILA's majestic moonlight collector, towering 6 stories high and 60 feet across, and weighing in at a healthy 25 tons.

Science enthusiast **Richard Chapin** conceived of the collector when a close friend was faced with a terminal illness. Chapin was intrigued by research on full-spectrum light therapy, which had been conducted mostly using artificial light sources.

Chapin wondered if the unique spectrum of moonlight might have been overlooked. The sublime lunar glow carries slightly different frequencies than sunlight, with more reds and yellows. It's no secret that moonlight is essential to a variety of life forms on Earth, but could it be used to aid the ailing?

Chapin collaborated with a crew of passionate engineers, telescope makers, and astronomers to design the collector. Comprised of 84 mirrored panels, each 4 feet by 8 feet, the "non-imaging optical array" is parabolic, hydraulic, and rotates 360

degrees with a mere 5hp motor. To weather the harsh desert conditions, the panels are made of a unique sandwich construction, with materials like aluminum honeycomb chosen for lightness, rigidity, and stability.

The collector is steered with amazing precision; the light can be focused on an area as small as 1mm or as large as 10 feet across. Due to the high volume of visitors, folks are allotted only a few minutes in its light, longer for those with serious illnesses.

Richard and his wife, **Monica Chapin**, are focused on promoting research and gaining scientific backing. They've worked with University of Arizona geoscientists who documented molecular changes in quartz crystals exposed to the collector for 45 minutes.

Believers abound, as witnessed by the exuberance of visitors and the testimonials on the ILA website. On any given full moon, folks from far and wide make the pilgrimage, hopeful that a solution could really be that simple, natural, and abundant.

—*Goli Mohammadi*

≫ **Interstellar Light Applications:** starlightuses.com

Stylish Change

Stacey Lee Webber likes her work long, repetitive, and painstaking. Just look at the life-sized carpenter's tools she silver-soldered out of pennies.

Only pre-1982 coins — minted from 95% copper — would survive her acetylene torch's high heat, so Webber spent hours flipping and sorting bucketfuls of mixed years.

"It's a mindless task to do while you're watching TV," she says. "I have a lot of those little tasks in my studio, it seems."

She spent months just twisting silver wire into the sheets of ornate filigree she used to build a set of jeweler's tools. When she moved on to screwdrivers, a hammer, and a handsaw, she meticulously cut her pennies (no, it's not illegal) and fused them together into panels with little gaps, so they rolled easily into the forms she desired. Darts cut in the flat swaths helped them to fold into the right shapes.

"A lot of the art is just figuring out the material and how to mold it into what I want," Webber explains. As she worked on the carpenter's tools, which showed this past August at San Francisco's Velvet da Vinci gallery, she says, "I was thinking about labor that my grandpa would understand, about how we value it, and about putting labor back into currency."

While preparing the pennies, she laid them between towels to shield the decorative textures of their faces from her hammer blows. For looks, she plated the finished objects lightly with copper and added a patina using liver of sulfur.

She confesses, however, that the final pieces are not as exciting for her as assembling them.

"The act of making something can be what a piece is about. That's why tools themselves keep standing out to me," she says, adding, "I love the penny — it's doing well for me."

—*Eric Smillie*

More Stylish Currency: staceyleewebber.com

Photograph by Studio M. Tom McInvaille

Planeboat Memories

It's a bird, it's a plane, it's a ... boat? Technically, it's a planeboat. And to **Dave Drimmer** of Fort Lauderdale, Fla., the live-aboard craft was home for 20 years.

The vessel has a colorful history. Its name, *Cosmic Muffin*, comes from singer Jimmy Buffett, who caught a glimpse of the yacht on a sailing trip and wrote it into his 1992 novel, *Where Is Joe Merchant?*

But the planeboat started out as infamous aviator Howard Hughes' personal Boeing 307 Stratoliner in 1939. Rumor has it Rita Hayworth had a hand in decorating its 12-foot-wide interior. In 1964, under different ownership in Florida, the plane was grounded by Hurricane Cleo.

It didn't stay on land for long. After buying it as scrap for $70 in 1969, the vehicle's new owner decided to salvage the ailing aircraft and turn it into a motor yacht. Then in 1981, current owner Drimmer answered an ad in the local classifieds: "Unique houseboat, great bachelor pad."

"It was in horrible condition and almost everyone tried to talk me out of buying it," Drimmer says, "but it had a strange and wonderful appeal that compelled me to grab it."

With trashed floors, a leaking, rotted hull, and no motors, propellers, or rudders to speak of, Drimmer had his work cut out for him just making the boat livable. With the help of friends, he stopped the leaks, rewired the electrical system, installed a water heater, air conditioning, and fridge, and renovated the head (that's bathroom in boatspeak). Powerful motors installed in recent years have made it seaworthy once again.

Drimmer lives on land these days, but the planeboat is docked nearby. He's always willing to give tours and charters, and to talk on and on about the strange conveyance he once called home. He kinda misses the old girl.

"My house doesn't move around at all," he says. "I really enjoyed the motion of the ocean. And being in a fuselage sometimes felt like flying."

—*Megan Mansell Williams*

>> **Now Boarding:** planeboats.com

Strike Anywhere

Teen firebug **Billy Gordon** knew what to do when he saw matches on sale at the supermarket. Buy 20,000 of them. And when he got them home? Use them to build one gigantic, strike-anywhere match.

He measured an ordinary 2¼-inch kitchen match with digital calipers, then scaled it up precisely to 8 feet. That meant he needed an explosive match head 7 inches long, laid on 1 inch thick.

"I've been doing pyrotechnical projects my entire life," says Gordon. At age 8 he dismantled fireworks and concocted new ones under parental supervision. By his teens he had taught himself to breathe fire, using kerosene or paraffin. His recent Instructables projects (screen name: Tetranitrate) include flash powder, thermite, exploding paint, an egg-timer detonator, "fire shaving" (mmm, burnt hair), and a really-not-advisable laser tattoo (mmm, burnt flesh).

Now 20, Gordon splits his time between his intern gig at Instructables HQ in San Francisco and NYU's Polytechnic Institute in Brooklyn, N.Y., where his studies in electrical engineering have sparked nonflammable projects like an LED chess set, hand-cranked Lego USB charger, and spy camera shirt.

To make the mighty match head, he spent weeks cutting the heads off 15,000 cardboard safety matches. He mixed in 30 ping-pong balls dissolved with acetone to make nitrocellulose glue, then glommed it all onto a 4×4 post. For the giant strike-anywhere tip, he snipped 250 wooden kitchen matches and glued those on top, one by one — risky business, as the slightest impact could have set the whole thing off. A little paint to brighten it up, and it was showtime.

When igniting the giant match, Gordon didn't actually singe off his eyebrows, but at least one reader felt compelled to ask. At a show-and-tell night for Instructables users, he swung the colossal firestarter against a sandpaper striker, detonating an unexpected 6-foot fireball that nearly forced him to drop the hot potato.

"For about a half-second I was thinking, 'Great, this works,' then it quickly went to, 'Crap, I might burn myself!'"

—*Keith Hammond*

🎥 **How-to and Video:** instructables.com/id/giant-match

Photograph by Noah Weinstein

Photograph by Alecia Ragan

Political Hot Seat

Here's a new look for your home that will have people discussing the politics of the day. **Sean Ragan** of Austin, Texas, created the Street Spam Lounger from campaign signs and other "street spam."

Ragan got the idea when he saw a flyer posted on a street pole by Citizens Against Ugly Street Spam (CAUSS) in 2001. The thought of creative reuse was appealing to him "not just for the usual environmental reasons," but also because he "likes to try to see the untapped potential in mundane, everyday items."

A graduate student studying organic chemistry, Ragan created the profile for the chair based on a design in James Hennessey and Victor Papanek's book *Nomadic Furniture*.

Made from corrugated plastic, the lounger is basically a cardboard chair. Each chair requires 21 "picket" signs measuring 18"×24", and one large 4'×8' "billboard" sign.

The four bulkheads that define the chair's profile are cut from the large sign; the skin covering the back and seat is made from the small signs, folded to slot into the bulkheads and provide rigidity. You can cut them by hand with a utility knife, but ideally they'd be die-cut and scored by machine.

Ragan's first prototype was completed at the beginning of 2002 and it definitely had people talking. "People are sometimes afraid to sit on it, but it's quite sturdy," he says.

Since election season is upon us, now is the perfect time for re-creating this lounger. When hunting for materials, Ragan recommends checking out your local campaign office to see if they have signs they're getting rid of.

"They'll probably be glad to give away all that people can carry off, once they're done with them," he advises. So come November, expect to see Street Spam Loungers everywhere.

—*Ed Troxell*

>> **Street Spam Lounger How-to:** makezine.com/go / spamlounger

Generated in Italy

Giorgio Olivero is fresh back from that digital fabrication workshop in Berlin — four months of work done in just ten 14-hour days!

Olivero is the tall, bony, curly-haired, gleaming-eyed creative director of TODO (todo.to.it), an up-and-coming Italian media design studio. Phones ring. Glossy magazines pile up. Olivero's studio is clad in bright, wriggly, digitally designed wallpaper. There's a huge plastic kiosk unplugged in the back room, the relic of a wealthy client.

Olivero punctuates his conversation by tapping cigarette ashes perilously near his keyboard. "Beyond the screen," he says, that's the way Marius Watz framed it, over there in Berlin, at the Transmediale. In tomorrow's world beyond the screen, software engineers will become product engineers. With digital 3D printers, of course. With CNC mills. Laser cutters. Yes!

Or maybe — Olivero is staring at the lozenges on the wall through his steely designer glasses — maybe it's really all about the *interaction* between the artist and the fabricator. Forget giving the device some super-intricate plan to cut — that's "boring" (a favorite Olivero term). Instead there's a man-machine dialogue there. An elegant language. A generative dialogue that makes stuff.

The digital control of numerical tools makes complexity so easy. You can cut a Mandelbrot set out of plywood if you're willing to sit around for a couple of years while the laser traces its endless fractal curls. But at the end, what have you made? Just a replica, not a truly original thing in itself. It's time to get past that old idea of fabs as "rapid prototype machines" and find something *unique to that design language*.

An interactive, semiautonomous pattern generation machine that makes real artifacts. Yes! They're here, they're now, they're almost cheap, and Olivero knows how to program them. He could generate random screen-saver patterns, throw a million designs at the wall like spaghetti, but no! Being Italian, being European, a craftsman, a human being, Olivero has to ask himself: what does it all *mean*?

Olivero's office is in downtown Torino, a city rife with the fruitily Baroque extravagances of royal Savoy architects. Guarino Guarini and Filippo Juvarra were mystical masons who piled ornaments together like conic sections of whipped cream. Weird mathematical structures, therefore, bore Olivero — been there, done that, in the late 1600s!

What's *interesting* is a computer reforming industrial production. The mass-produced assembly line stripped away decor and ornament. It stripped away the handcrafted parts of the Italian city landscape, too. But here comes the computer to *restore* decoration and ornament — not the old-fashioned William Morris kind, of wallpaper so full of little birds and vines that it makes your eyes bleed, but *unprecedented* decoration and ornament. The 21st-century kind!

Take — Olivero points over a colleague's head as the guy pounds away manfully at his screen — take that module, there! Decoration and ornament are made from modules. Modules are elements of a repeating pattern changed in harmonious ways — flipped, rotated, inverted, tiled — you can do that by hand, and that's easy to program, but what's *really* interesting is *a new language* for doing that. How?

The mass-produced assembly line stripped away decor and ornament. But here comes the computer to *restore* them.

An old Arts and Crafts decorator, like Morris, went out into Nature like a good Pre-Raphaelite, to copy, say, a grapevine, and then extracted graphic elements of that grapevine into something human hands could make.

But that's so over! So what if — Olivero digs around for an overstuffed graphics file on his screen and pops it open — what if you start *abstracting the math behind the growth of vines* instead? You map growth patterns, constraints, the basic forces ... then you can generate *digitally varying* modules of ornament, you "escape the module" with a process that generates decorative objects! And with industrial value!

We're studying an interwoven black-and-white

ESCAPING THE MODULE: Designer Giorgio Olivero's algorithmically germinated creations are locally grown, laser-harvested, and hand-assembled in Italy.

checkerboard that has exploded into a basket of tendrils. It's a glossy, writhing cylinder fringed like an electrified straw hat.

It also looks Italian. Somehow. Definitely. It's a brand-new object that frankly looks like nothing else on Earth, but I've been in Italy quite a while now and this fabject definitely looks Italian. Gina Lollobrigida looks less Italian than this newly generated thing.

"Melting plastic isn't enough any more!" Olivero declares with infectious glee. Conventional industrial design is collapsing in Europe, the assembly lines are all heading for China, and there's a tidal wave of design grads coming out of the schools! Meanwhile, Italy's dotted all over with small tech companies with exquisitely high-end digital equipment, and they're not using their full production capacity!

So that makes sense, but just one problem there. Nobody's got a clue how to talk to machines with their own digital tools.

What this situation calls for are some real software engineers with skills and sensibilities. Arduino chip guys! Computational aesthetic Processing gods like Reas and Fry and Marius Watz! They're digital artists making one-of-a-kind fine-art sculptures, electronic art you can *feed right into the fine art market*, collectible, beautiful!

That's the new horizon! Because it's organically grown out of the computer graphics world, the interaction design world, and you can print it out and put it right there on the table next to the olive oil! It's a real-time sculptural medium with static pieces that have kinetic value — no, they've got *use value*, they might even turn out to be *industrially practical*!

Or maybe — Olivero says it with a sophisticate's shrug — maybe it's all a collective hallucination.

So, as the creative director of his growing young firm, does he jump on that train, or not? That's the question.

And that's not a *boring* question. That's *interesting*.

Bruce Sterling is a science fiction writer and was the guest curator of the SHARE Festival 2007 in Torino, Italy.

Bring DIY Inspiration to a Kid You Don't Know

Beginning this summer, the Maker Media team began taking the magic of MAKE on the road — literally. Funded in part by a grant from IBM, we're converting a 1981 Mercedes fire truck, dubbed the MakeMobile, into a mobile workshop that will pay visits to economically challenged schools in our Northern California backyard. The MakeMobile is equipped with everything we need to inspire students with demonstrations and hands-on workshops in an almost endless variety of science and technology areas — from circuit building and robotics to kites, automata, and mechanical toys.

Our goal is simple: to bring a hands-on DIY experience to kids who often lack sufficient exposure to, and mentoring in, science and technology. We hope to build on this pilot program to inspire and support MakeMobiles and Maker Mentor teams in other communities throughout the world.

The MakeMobile is just one example of how when you subscribe to MAKE you're doing more than quenching your own thirst for DIY inspiration: you're supporting a growing constellation of maker communities and educators dedicated to mentoring students of all ages, nationalities, and economic circumstances.

This past year MAKE (and our sister magazine CRAFT) provided financial and promotional support to dozens of educational programs worldwide; from Science Olympiad (soinc.org) and the Tech Challenge (techchallenge.thetech.org), to Vision Ed's Robofest in New York City (visionedinc.org/robofest) and Education Day at our own Maker Faire (makerfaire. com), where we bused in hundreds of middle school and high school students to drink from the same DIY fountain that inspires the rest of us as MAKE editors, contributors, and subscribers.

It shouldn't come as a surprise to anyone who has read MAKE that we're primarily a circulation-based magazine. We deeply appreciate the support of our sponsors and advertisers, but by design our primary financial support is from subscribers. This means you won't find "practically free" subscription offers in an attempt to inflate our rate base for advertisers.

Our goal is simple: to bring a hands-on DIY experience to kids who often lack sufficient exposure to science and technology.

We simply can't keep the quality of the magazine up to our readers' standards if we do that.

Nonetheless, this spring we introduced a special subsidized teacher's rate of just $19.95/year when a subscription is delivered to a school address. If you know a school or teacher who might value a gift subscription, we're happy to extend this special rate to gift-givers as well. We've posted details on how to give at makezine.com/school.

The word *membership* is often overused by companies trying to confer a sense of privilege to their customers. In the case of MAKE, however, your subscription is as much a pledge as a member of the maker community as it is a magazine subscription.

The same goes for our loyal advertisers. You don't wear your membership badge on your sleeve, but you are tied together by your generosity as well as your curiosity. And for this, we salute you.

Our pledge in return is to continue to seek out and support programs that will spread the passion, spirit, and knowledge of makers through student mentorship and educational programs worldwide.

Dan Woods is associate publisher of MAKE and CRAFT magazines.

Photograph by Scott Beale

Make:
television

DIY Projects with John Park

Featuring Makers and More Makers

GRAB YOUR REMOTE!
(If you haven't already made it into a project.)

MAKE: The new Public Television series **premieres in January 2009.**

» **makezine.tv**

YOU BUILD IT, THEY WILL WATCH!

Submit your video and you can be on **Make: television.**

» **makerchannel.org**

Germs on a Plane

The Scenario: Imagine you're a world-renowned epidemiologist (yeah, we know it's a stretch, but just roll with it). You're on your way back home to Northern California from a pandemics conference in Tokyo, with your 5-year-old child and significant other, cruising over the Pacific at 37,000 feet, and at least six more hours from home — or any airport, for that matter.

You've had your second meal and watched the movie, and you're dozing peacefully in your business class seat when your child wakes you to say he really needs to use the bathroom. So you get up to escort him to the nearest lav, only to run into the longest lines of passengers you've ever seen waiting to get to all of the plane's restrooms, from first class to coach.

An anxious flight attendant tries to push past you carrying numerous loaded barf bags as you stop her to ask what's going on. Trying to remain calm, she says that, unless you're a doctor, could you please return to your seat. Well, as fate would have it....

The Challenge: Clearly there's an outbreak of unknown origin spreading through the plane, and the sense of panic is starting to build among the passengers and flight crew. Given your credentials, you might be the only person that everyone, including the captain, will listen to. So, putting aside all your years of medical school and practice for the moment — since a snap diagnosis might do as much harm as good — what are you going to do to manage the crisis?

What You Have: In addition to the airliner's basic emergency medical supplies, you have whatever any of the passengers might be carrying on a commercial aircraft capable of trans-oceanic flight. And, for the purposes of this challenge, you can assume the flight crew and passengers will follow your instructions without argument, be they very old, very young, or anyone who had significant health issues prior to boarding the plane. So ... what now, Doc?

Send a detailed description of your MakeShift solution with sketches and/or photos to makeshift@makezine.com by Nov. 21, 2008. If duplicate solutions are submitted, the winner will be determined by the quality of the explanation and presentation. The most plausible and most creative solutions will each win a MAKE T-shirt and a MAKE Pocket Reference. Think positive and include your shirt size and contact information with your solution. Good luck! For readers' solutions to previous MakeShift challenges, visit makezine.com/makeshift.

And the next MakeShift challenge could be yours! That's right, we're throwing open the doors and offering you the chance to create your own MakeShift to challenge the world. Just submit an original scenario in the familiar format — the challenge, what you have, etc. — with some ideas of how you think it should be solved. The winning scenario will not only be published right here but also earn you a $50 gift certificate for the Maker Shed. The deadline is Nov. 21, 2008, so get out there and start looking for trouble!

Lee D. Zlotoff is a writer/producer/director among whose numerous credits is creator of MacGyver. He is also president of Custom Image Concepts (customimageconcepts.com).

Photograph by Jen Siska

Maker

Bend It Like Bach

Tim Kaiser's fabulously weird world of music.

By Karen K. Hansen

When English soccer star David Beckham bends the ball, the international sports world watches in awe. When American musician Tim Kaiser bends a circuit, the audience listens just as intently, be it in an art or performance space, or a bar, bookstore, or library.

MAKE, Volume 12 (*page 14*) introduced readers to Tim Kaiser, but even people who've never heard of him have probably heard his sounds. These may emanate from the instruments Kaiser himself creates and plays, such as Bungee Drums made from concrete post forms or the New Metal Violin made out of the battery compartment of a minesweeper. Or they may issue forth as distorted or modulated samples from one of Kaiser's Atomic SonicFX Boxes in the hands of other artists.

Among those emitting Kaiser sounds are Duran Duran and film score producer BT (Brian Transeau), who recently featured some of Kaiser's instruments in his recording *This Binary Universe*.

Photography by Matt Blum

Maker

CORDS AND CHORDS

As cutting-edge as Kaiser's work is, it's rooted in musical and technical fundamentals ranging from Franz Joseph Haydn, who evoked a ticking clock, to Reed Ghazala, who first bent a circuit.

Kaiser learned how things are made by fixing them. During high school he was a guitarist in what he calls Northern Minnesota's first punk rock band. "We were all broke, and the equipment we had was crappy, so we had to learn to fix our own stuff."

Contending with an amplifier that routinely overheated, Kaiser thought, "In junior high I learned how to solder. Why couldn't I just cut a hole in the back and put a fan in there?" No wonder he still considers basic electrical and soldering skills "super-valuable" for makers.

He cites an early realization that a manufacturer's delay pedal with just 2 seconds of delay was more about production costs than possibilities. By changing a few potentiometers, Kaiser increased the delay to 4 seconds. The internal workings of many of his devices result from swapping out components to make something more versatile. "I'm Mr. Void-the-Warranty," he says. "People who know how to do things with their hands are the ones who make the world better."

Kaiser often tries to re-create a real-world tone that resonates with him — such as the sound of a train braking while the Doppler effect lowers the pitch. That makes him heir to avant-garde musicians John Cage and Nicolas Collins, who used "found sound" electronically, and to traditional composers such as Vivaldi, Beethoven, and Saint-Saëns, who orchestrated sounds of dogs and bones, birds and storms.

Kaiser begins compositions by improvising with a tape running. He then scores the parts he likes so he can replicate them in performance. As he composes, Kaiser doesn't consciously employ traditional musical elements such as motifs and variations, but he hears them in his finished works.

SOLDER AND SOUNDS

When making instruments, Kaiser sometimes starts from scratch or from scrap foraged from yard sales and salvage yards. Other times he transforms traditional instruments.

OLD PLUS OLD EQUALS NEW: Kaiser merges a violin with scrap to produce a unique instrument.

His background in guitar and music theory came into play when he turned a simple dulcimer into a cello — sort of. When he changed the distance between the nut and the bridge, the scale was no longer diatonic. He pulled the frets and smoothed the fingerboard, then replaced the three dulcimer strings with cello strings. But, because the body was small, the modified dulcimer lacked a cello's deep resonance. Naturally, Kaiser's response was to plug it into something.

Cue the piezoelectric transducer. Kaiser attaches piezos to all his instruments that start out acoustic and become electronic. Inexpensive and versatile, piezos are little metal disks with a special ceramic inside. Apply pressure to them and they output voltage. Apply signal and they output vibration.

If you know how to solder, Kaiser says, it's simple to wire piezos to a circuit or a jack, or to add a volume knob. He uses poster putty to test placement and two-step epoxy to affix piezos permanently.

One of Kaiser's commissions came from Shawn, a heavy-metal guitarist in California (he

LIGHT MUSIC:
In Tim Kaiser's ears
and hands, the tines
of a candleholder base
become a musical
instrument.

THE SOUND OF SERENDIPITY: "I'm a firm believer in discovering something while you are in the process of looking for something else."

prefers not to give a surname). Now in a wheelchair, Shawn can no longer do the "spandex jumping-up-and-down-on-stage thing." Asked to amplify Shawn's autoharp and make it look cool, Kaiser replaced the soundboard with diamond plate, installed pickups, and added blinking lights and a Buick "Special" emblem. He also built FX units that Shawn's Atomic AutoHarp plugs into for distortion and delay. Kaiser is sure it sounds "fantastically hellacious."

When Kaiser had the Atomic AutoHarp on his workbench, his creative fancy turned to thoughts of piano harps, then zithers. Ultimately he created the Newport Custom for his own performances. It sounds like a "prepared piano" and beats hauling a baby grand to gigs.

That's typical of Kaiser's openness to experimenting and letting things evolve. "I'm a firm believer in discovering something while you are in the process of looking for something else."

As he was building a tall, stringed instrument to be played with mallets — fashioned from piano hammers sunk into drumsticks — his violin bow fell onto the workbench. "Ah," he thought,

"It's a bass!" He now plays that Upright Spring Bass exclusively with a bow.

In Kaiser's ears and hands, almost anything can become a musical instrument. He got funny looks at a Goodwill store when he plucked the tines of a candleholder base and "they really resonated." That 49-cent object became the JuJuBe, which Kaiser plays by running a violin bow around the tines and sending the sound through a modulation delay. "If I've got the right soundman, I can really rattle the windows."

BENT, NOT BROKEN

Kaiser's scorecard doesn't track fame or fortune: "I'm as famous as I deserve to be, and I don't need to be stinkin' rich. I've got kids and a beautiful wife, and a nice house. I'm always looking for the next interesting thing, and it's that process that gives me fulfillment."

➕ Kaiser's website: timkaiser.org

Based in Minneapolis, Karen K. Hansen is a writer and clarinetist, of the classical ilk.

Photography by Kyle George

Solar-Powered Studio

Bruce Baldwin's DIY desert dream. By Charles Platt

Drive a couple hundred miles east from Los Angeles along Interstate 40, and you enter the high desert of Northern Arizona, where each small town is separated from the next by 30 or 40 miles of wilderness. Take an exit past an extinct volcano named Picacho Butte, and you find yourself on a rutted dirt road winding among junipers and red rocks. There's no power out here, no phone lines, and no water. The primary residents are rattlesnakes and jackrabbits — yet when you turn onto another road that's barely a track, you find, of all things, a solar-powered recording studio.

Audio quality that might have cost $1 million 20 years ago can be bought for maybe $10,000 today. Instead of laying down a 64-track master using Ampex tape decks the size of cooking stoves, you save to a hard drive. Mixing, EQ, and effects can be done with software, and by collaborating through the web, a bass player in Los Angeles can add a track to a beat that was recorded in New York — or in the Arizona wilderness. Even out here, a cellular connection enables internet access at 1.5Mbps. That's fast enough to swap .wav files.

Bruce Baldwin didn't foresee all this when he started building his little studio, but he's not surprised. What other people regard as happy coincidences, he sees as "symbiotic catalysm." He insists that "if you have a specific purpose and are pursuing it with a passion, you will be drawn to people, material — and most importantly, knowledge — to make it occur. I have minimal construction abilities, but by relying on the structure itself to guide me through every step of the process, everything fit exactly the way it was supposed to."

Formerly a technician and field engineer for a now-defunct major defense contractor, Baldwin

ECO ENGINEER: Baldwin in the studio, taking a break from editing tracks recorded by Grand Canyon Railroad singer Joe Pronto.

There are no neighbors and no law enforcement to tell people to turn their amps down.

reconsidered his vocation during the first Gulf War. "I became disenchanted by weapons people," he says, "when I saw them celebrating that their system worked because it successfully targeted a hospital door." Aged 37, he abandoned his house, put together his savings, bought a motor home, and spent the next seven years on the road.

Finally an Arizona real estate agent showed him slightly more than 40 acres for a mere $22,000. "She made me walk up the hill with my eyes closed," he recalls. "When I opened my eyes I found I had a 60-mile view to the east, and 40 miles to the west."

The location was right, and he liked the climate, so he parked his RV and started a small business installing solar power equipment for others like himself who wanted to live off the grid. A couple years later he decided to begin building.

Since Baldwin had never tried construction work, he started by reading books to find out how to do it. The one he liked best was *Practical Pole Building Construction* by Leigh Seddon. "I wanted a method that I could use completely and totally by myself," he recalls. "I looked into straw-bale, Rastra, many options, but all of them were labor intensive and needed a lot of people. In pole building, an entire

house can be supported on just 20 poles, and the rest of the structure goes up one stick at a time." His initial studio space needed only six poles.

Baldwin rented a Bobcat with an auger attachment to drill the holes, each 1 foot in diameter and 4 feet deep. He poured hand-mixed concrete into each hole and set a 4×6 pressure-treated Douglas-fir post into the concrete. He attached joists between these poles, laid plywood as a floor, then put in rafters and added a roof.

Now he had protection from the weather as he set about installing the walls. He used bolts to attach all the structural members. The only time he needed help was when he installed ceiling panels: he couldn't hold them up and screw them into place at the same time.

Since there were no formal building inspections at that time in his corner of the wilderness, he was free to construct the studio as he wished. Still, he says, it would meet or exceed all codes, including factors such as winter snow loads on the roof.

He bought lumber from the usual sources, but saved money on windows and doors by taking advantage of a policy that he found at Lowe's stores in Phoenix. Anytime a customer returned something that was special-ordered, the store put it out on the floor at a heavily reduced clearance price. "There are 13 Lowe's stores in Phoenix," according to Baldwin. "I went to every one of them."

Construction took longer than he expected, but he only worked on it part time (sometimes as little as one weekend in a month). As he refined the interior, he found himself getting into fine wood finishing. The whole process took three years.

On the roof are seven solar panels yielding about 800 watts. The primary inverter, providing 120 volts AC, is an Exeltech, which generates pure sine-wave output.

"They're mil-spec," Baldwin explains, "used in every war room, submarine, and battleship, normally $5,000 but I picked it up for $1,000. It arrived packed in acoustical foam, which of course was very useful to me." There it was again: symbiotic catalysm at work. The universe was giving him exactly what he needed.

ABOVE: AGM battery bank stores solar power for the studio, while a banjo provides inspiration to visiting cowboy poets. RIGHT: Power center contains all the equipment needed for off-grid electrical generation.

Baldwin has a Tascam mixing board, JBL monitors, a MIDI keyboard, and a Dell dual-Pentium PC running Cakewalk Sonar Producer Edition as his primary software. He runs Rode and Shure microphones through an Aphex 107 preamp "which is obsolete but produces a slightly warmer sound." He can save onto DAT (half-inch digital audiotape cassettes), although this too is becoming obsolete.

The wilderness location provides a unique benefit: total silence outside, without even a twitter of bird-song. Baldwin adjusts the resonance in his studio simply by opening the windows. Also, there's the aesthetic payoff. "When you're trying to sing an inspiring song," he says, "you can be looking at a beautiful view instead of facing a cloth drape with a concrete wall behind it."

The entire project cost less than $50,000, including construction materials (some of them scrounged and salvaged), solar-electric equipment, studio electronics, and the price of the land.

Although he pursued the project primarily for himself, he's willing to advise others on what he learned (email him at solarstudio2001@hotmail.com) and one day he may consider opening the studio to artists he admires who would enjoy the beauty of the location.

> There it was again: symbiotic catalysm at work. The universe was giving him exactly what he needed.

"I have a nice little campground at the bottom of the hill," he says. "They can do what they like out here. There are no neighbors and no law enforcement to tell people to turn their amps down. I even have a perfect natural amphitheater for live performances."

Of course, people will have to do some driving to get there. The nearest town, population 1,000, is ten miles away. And Baldwin may be away on business for a while. He was recently named head coach of the U.S. floor hockey team for the 2009 Special Olympics World Winter Games in Idaho.

But since symbiotic catalysm provided Baldwin with his studio, he has no doubt that when the time is right, visitors will be able to find it.

Charles Platt is a contributing editor to MAKE.

1 IN 6 BILLION: Beatrice and father Hugh in his home office, where he searched her DNA for clues to her unique condition.

My Daughter's DNA

One father's search for the scientific answers that no one seemed to have. By Hugh Young Rienhoff Jr.

If you scrape the inside of your cheek with a popsicle stick and mix it with a few homely salts and a shot of grain alcohol, you'll see a fluffy cloud of material floating in the glass. It looks like cotton, but it's really the code of you. DNA is deceptively ordinary-looking.

The human genome — the totality of each person's genes within their body — is a vast chemical space with 6.6 billion bits of DNA information that constitutes genetically what we are as *Homo sapiens*. In that vastness, it's easy for a single deviant bit of DNA to hide. I suspected that, like many of those with genetic conditions, my daughter also had a single DNA base that was awry. Finding that variant is like looking for a single person in a world of 6 billion people. It's a near-impossible task unless you have clues for where to look, for which genes might be

altered. Clues like this always begin with the patient.

The Birth of Beatrice

My wife and I purposely avoided learning the sex of our third pregnancy, in part to add to the drama of delivery: we wanted to be surprised. I stood by Lisa as she lay on the table; though I am a physician, I could never become accustomed to the sight of the birth of my own children. As my daughter emerged, I caught a glimpse of her before she was wrapped in the towel and thought: what long feet you have!

Physicians can be like ornithologists glimpsing *rara avis*, and those feet reminded me of Marfan syndrome — a genetic condition that also imparts a tall and lanky frame. I had never seen an infant with that condition, and this was neither the time nor place for me to be a doctor. I began to cry as

Photograph by Cody Pickens

I had at the birth of my two boys; I stroked Lisa's hair and wiped her cheeks, thanking her for such a beautiful girl.

The hospital pediatrician examined Beatrice and approached me asking if there were any family history of congenital abnormalities. "No," I said. She explained: Beatrice has a birthmark on her face and her fingers and toes are bent half-closed, contracted. She called it nevus flammeus and arthrogryposis. These were new words for me.

Who Knows More?

The next few weeks took us to a host of physicians — orthopedic surgeons, geneticists, neurologists. There are three questions patients ask of doctors: what do I have, what can I do about it, and who can help me. The first question is the most important. With a diagnosis comes a prognosis, a vision of the future based on past cases. A diagnosis also suggests how to manage the case: what tests need to be done routinely, what unseen issues need close watching. A diagnosis can also dictate treatment. Finally, a diagnosis can lead you to the expert who's experienced in managing patients with the condition.

We had a diagnosis. In fact, we had four or five. But none of them stuck. Each specialist seemed to focus on "their system" but in each instance my daughter did not fit neatly into any category. True, she had some features of Marfan syndrome, with her long, beautiful fingers and flat, narrow feet. But the whites of her eyes were eggshell blue and her muscles were underdeveloped — these did not fit. She had nothing recognizable, no syndrome that could account for the constellation of findings.

Despite the successful sequencing of the human genome, the diagnosis of genetic conditions is more often based on the history of the patient's problems, their family history, and a complete physical examination. The exam is key: genetic conditions generally affect many different systems of the body. Some physical signs are obvious, like small stature or mental retardation. But others are subtle, such as the patterns of the thumbprint, and require a well-trained and inquisitive eye. It's the concurrence of various findings that can cinch a diagnosis.

Although Beatrice had been seen by at least a dozen physicians, what she really needed was a thorough physical exam. This became more urgent as her weakness became more obvious and as she failed to gain weight. I quietly urged her physicians to perform that exam. Everybody was very busy, more focused on the immediate issues of weight and feeding, bones or muscle. In truth, few physicians today perform such an examination, in which they note the position of the ears, look deep into the eyes, examine fingerprints, and measure the fingers and limbs. The full physical exam is becoming a lost art.

So I took Beatrice to my alma mater. I was trained at the Johns Hopkins Hospital in internal medicine and adult clinical genetics. Hopkins is known for its expertise in Marfan syndrome.

After examining Bea in the Hopkins genetics clinic, Dr. David Valle and his colleagues seemed to recognize what was wrong. They pointed out that Bea's uvula — the small piece of flesh hanging in the back of the throat — was forked and that Bea's eyes were spaced more widely than usual. They called another physician who examined the same features. They nodded knowingly the way doctors do among themselves. They asked for DNA. Beatrice bravely offered her arm to the phlebotomist.

> DNA sequencing has become a prosaic laboratory routine. The necessary equipment can be had on eBay for $2,000. Thus, I undertook to study my daughter's DNA.

At the end of the visit, one of the physicians who examined Bea handed me a paper published three weeks earlier describing a new syndrome, Loeys-Dietz syndrome (LDS). He was the lead author. On the plane home, I read about the characteristics of this new syndrome: forked uvula, widely spaced eyes, and devastating vascular disease affecting the aorta. Average age of death: 27. This is not the diagnosis I wanted.

My Own Hypothesis

Now began a waiting game. An echocardiogram showed the aorta was normal; the genes associated with the new syndrome were normal in Bea. It appeared Bea did not have LDS. Everyone was stumped. Come back next year, they advised.

I read the LDS paper and then a newer paper,

each many times. I read all the references. A year passed, during which I slowly got a grip on the new thinking regarding Marfan syndrome and LDS. I learned that the manifestations of Marfan syndrome and LDS were thought to arise from an overactive biochemical pathway involving a hormone called TGF-beta. Though Bea did not appear to have Marfan syndrome or LDS, she clearly had something similar to those conditions.

The hormone and receptors implicated in Marfan syndrome and LDS were very closely related to a hormone that regulates muscle cell size and number. This pathway had not been implicated in human disease, but the three related genes seemed like obvious candidates to harbor a variant that could cause small, weak muscles.

Though many experts in the field were willing to discuss the idea, none were willing to examine these genes in Bea. It was unclear why: Was the hypothesis too weak? Were the liabilities too great? For me and for Bea, I felt compelled, so I proceeded to do it myself.

Doing My Own DNA Work

It had been 15 years since I had sequenced DNA, so I was surprised to learn that it had become a prosaic laboratory routine. Indeed, most researchers prepare the DNA and send it to a contract laboratory. It is straightforward to set up such an experiment. The reagents are cheap and the procedures for preparing the sequencing reactions are widely available; the entire reference human genome can be found in public domain databases such as GenBank and Ensembl; and the necessary equipment can be had on eBay for $2,000. Thus, I undertook to test my hypothesis and study my daughter's DNA.

A gene is sequenced piecemeal, 300 to 500 nucleotides at a time. Each of the genes I studied in Beatrice was about 5,000 nucleotides long. The DNA sequence for each segment is emailed from the lab as a single file called a chromatogram, which shows the color-coded nucleotides at each position along the gene (as shown on page 43).

I reviewed each file after the children were asleep, with the house quiet. Not trusting the software to identify every nucleotide correctly, I examined every peak of the chromatogram. It is tedious work, and I feared I might overlook the answer. Each nucleotide of Bea's sequence was compared to the reference human genome sequence. It was eerie examining her DNA, as though I were peering through a powerful microscope looking deep into my daughter while

Understanding the Phenotype

Marfan syndrome is a heritable disease of connective tissues characterized by the presence of long limbs, toes, and fingers; dislocated lenses in the eyes; and aortic root dilatation. This collection of findings is called the *phenotype*.

A phenotype is any observable or measurable trait, such as the color of the iris, the number of scalp hairs per square centimeter, or even the amount of RNA transcription a given gene produces. In short, a phenotype is any observation that can be attributed in whole or in part to the action of genes. Included in the phenotype might be a person's response to medicine, longevity, or the course of a disease.

Phenotypes can be remarkably constant — each case of achondroplastic dwarfism, the most common genetic cause of short stature, closely resembles another, almost as if all achondroplasts were related. On the other hand, phenotypes can vary considerably. Patients with some forms of hereditary cancer can follow very different clinical paths.

she patiently lay on the microscope stage, looking up, hoping for answers.

Other Needles in the Haystack

In reviewing all the sequences for each of her three genes, I found that Bea had many of the normal variations documented in the genome database. And in critical regions of those genes, where I suspected the variant might lie, all appeared normal. I did, however, find one change not reported in any of the databases. And the change was in a location likely to regulate the activity of the gene.

Finding an unreported nucleotide change is just the beginning of a long phase of research to prove that the variant is responsible for the clinical findings. Most often this comes from identifying patients who share these signs and symptoms as well as a similar change in the gene. I asked many physicians if they had seen any other patients similar to Bea. None had.

Recognizing that Bea had something very rare if not unique, I decided to offer the world her story. I launched mydaughtersdna.org with the hope that other cases might surface. I designed the site so that any patient might publish their difficult or unique case, so that they too might benefit from the world of geneticists, scientists, and interested persons. While there have been no other reports of Beatrices, a dozen other mystery cases have been posted. The quality of the comments and suggestions is extremely high and is yet another testament to the wisdom of the web and its users. Most importantly, for one young woman, users of the site solved her case.

My goal as a father and as a reluctant scientist was to arrive at a diagnosis, which in turn might provide a prognosis and a treatment. Though there is no certainty I am on the right path, in thinking Bea's problem through, I believe I am very close to crafting, with her doctor, a clinical management plan. With the tentative understanding that she has something akin to Marfan and LDS, her biggest risk must be vascular disease. Thus the most important dictate is to have her aorta monitored yearly. I am also lucky because there is now a treatment that has helped forestall vascular disease in severe Marfan patients. Bea is on that medicine.

What I Learned

All of us experience medical challenges directly or indirectly. When we are on the edge, our hope lies in the fact that medical science is in motion and constantly revising itself. The theories I was taught about Marfan syndrome 20 years ago have been totally eclipsed by ideas that not only seem durable but also bring with them new hope for patients, in the form of treatment. This is also true for many other conditions. My experience confirmed the value of patient persistence.

I reaffirmed for myself the value of the simple things. Insisting on the low-tech but thorough physical exam, when more complicated and invasive tests were being suggested, proved crucial. I never lost sight that Bea has her limits in what she can tolerate in the way of finger pokes, needle sticks, and biopsies.

As a father I'm charged with protecting her as much as I am with helping her. Much of this is common sense, but that seems easy to lose in the anxiety of concern and the fog of ignorance.

More importantly I overcame a host of fears. It might have been easier to capitulate to the experts and accept their counsel of patience until science caught up with Bea. I certainly risked the ridicule of the experts. Scientists tire quickly of blackboard hypotheses, and though many were generous with their knowledge, a few with whom I spoke had no time for my ideas or questions.

But my curiosity could not be quenched; my skepticism could not be squelched. And the father in me trumped any shame that I might be wrong or concern that I was wasting time.

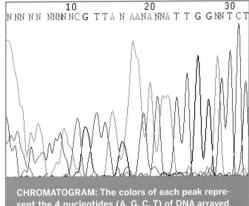

CHROMATOGRAM: The colors of each peak represent the 4 nucleotides (A, G, C, T) of DNA arrayed linearly in each of the 2 chromosomes. This figure shows the beginning of a gene sequence, where there is much ambiguity.

What We Learn

To be a patient or the parent of a patient is to be continually searching. Each of us does what is within our limits; my work on Bea's behalf is what any parent would do. We've entered an extraordinary era in which knowledge is exploding and is better distributed, where questioning the authorities is more accepted, and in which the "wisdom of the crowd" is at hand.

But it is vital to remind ourselves that with our surfeit of knowledge there is still a dearth of understanding. Though historically genetics has been focused on the rare and unusual, and dominated by a handful of experts, the new wave of understanding of the human genome cannot happen without our large-scale participation. Despite some protests from the academy, each of us has something very important to contribute to human genomics research: our DNA and our phenotype. It is perhaps the most profound experiment humankind will undertake to understand itself as a species.

⊞ More about Bea Rienhoff's case and others: mydaughtersdna.org

» Human Genome Project: genome.gov

Dedicated to the memory of Dr. Victor A. McKusick (1921–2008).

Hugh Young Rienhoff Jr. is a physician and entrepreneur in the San Francisco Bay Area.

Secret of Evermor

Flight of fancy on a monumental scale.
By Buzz Moran

Five miles south of Baraboo, Wis., across the highway from an abandoned ammunition plant, lie the larger-than-life sculptures of Dr. Evermor, a visionary Machine Age inventor who is the alter ego of retired salvage dealer Tom Every. I spoke with Every, who, despite being 70 and in a wheelchair, is still adding to the collection.

Buzz Moran: How did this work begin?
Dr. Evermor: It came out of a time of duress in my life, when I was unhappy. I built the Forevertron [the central sculpture] to get me the hell away from this planet. I'll climb inside that glass ball at the top, shoot it at the heavens, and make it back to the Lord on a magnetic lightning force beam.

I looked around at what I had to work with, and zam-zam, that's how it evolved. I started with a giant autoclave from the Apollo missions that weighed 32,000 pounds. Later I got ahold of some actual bipolar dynamos that Mr. Edison made, from the Ford museum, and stuck those in there.

Then I had to put a big 40-foot telescope nearby, so any doubting Thomases could see if the damn fool made it or not. Using the 1890s as a time frame, I added an elevated teahouse where Queen Victoria and Prince Albert would have sat and witnessed the launch. My family is all from England.

Another machine is the Graviton. When you're getting ready to go up and you're burly like me, you stand in that and *bzzzt*, it dewaters you to get you down to the right weight. That piece was an old X-ray machine. I also added an overlord master control tower, which I got up about 42 feet. I'd like to finish that up before I check out, you know?

Photography by Buzz and Cheryl Moran, and by Lauren Rauk (bottom right)

And then, oh, we've got to have a symphony out here. So I built a 70-piece bird band. You just keep adding things ...

BM: Your pieces often look like Victorian machines that were built for a specific purpose.
DE: I don't impose any kind of historic integrity to the forms. I just keep the energy flowing. I'll move pieces of whatever it might be, and they'll say, "You look plenty good to me, honey. Would you like to be next to me for the rest of your life?" So I'll put a little spot weld down there, and who's getting married to whom, you know? That's the way you've got to look at it, with that kind of humor.

BM: What are your current plans for the park?
DE: I'd like to just figure out where to set it down before I check out. I'd give the sculptures to anyone who would preserve them. There's no mortgages, no banks, no governments involved in the damn thing, so just plunk it over there, and if somebody puts a meter on it and makes a lot of money, that's fine. If you've got any suggestions I'm open to hearing 'em!

FACING PAGE: A small part of the very large Forevertron. THIS PAGE, CLOCKWISE FROM TOP LEFT: The Celestial Listening Ear; being dewatered in the Graviton; Dr. Evermor (pictured at left) and a visitor.

📷 See more photos at makezine.com/15/evermore.

Buzz Moran lives in Austin, Texas. He performs a show called Foleyvision, wherein bizarre foreign films are shown with all of the sound effects, voices, and music performed live in the theater. He is 6'1".

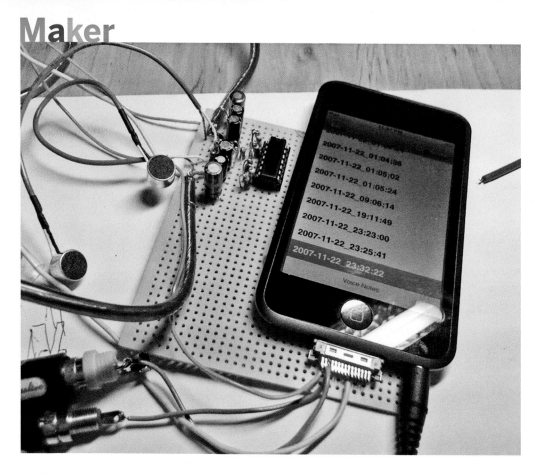

VoIPing the iPod Touch

How makers gave you the feature that Apple held back.

By Erica Sadun

It's a maker's dream: turn your homebrew ideas into a concrete reality and then ship that product. This dream came true for iPod hackers Dr. Marián Képesi, "Eok," and Samuel Vinson. They designed, built, and shipped an iPod touch microphone and developed VoIP (voice over internet protocol) software to place phone calls using that mic.

Last November, Képesi was poking around on his iPod Touch. A postdoc at Austria's Graz University of Technology, he had previously worked with third-generation iPods and was interested in the new Touch line.

During his explorations, he discovered an important fact about the iPod Touch's bottom connector port: its line-in audio was active. Live pins meant that the iPod Touch could connect to an external audio source. It was compatible with recording or,

better yet, with VoIP for talking over the internet. VoIP compatibility was a long-standing goal of the iPhone and iPod Touch hacker community.

Képesi modded an old iPod docking cable, connecting the line-in pins to live audio, and recorded his first sample. The sound level was very low but the signal was live. Although Apple had shipped the iPod Touch as a "play only" device, Képesi had uncovered its ability to record.

He announced his discovery on the iPod Touch fan forums, and set to work adding an amplifier and boosting the audio-in quality. It took some searching but he finally found a small microphone that would fit inside a standard iPod dock connector.

Képesi then put together his parts list and posted the circuit details so anyone could build the open source, dockable microphone. Together, the parts

Photograph by Marián Képesi

cost less than 20 euros— about 30 bucks.

Many intrepid makers used these instructions to build their own microphones but many didn't, or more realistically, couldn't. Between the fine-detail soldering and the extremely tight space considerations for the dock connector, iPod Touch fans begged Képesi for a pre-built solution. He handcrafted several more microphones for online acquaintances, but the time investment was prohibitive.

"Ridax" (home.swipnet.se/ridax) is a hobbyist in Sweden who frequents the iPodLinux forum. In 2005, Ridax began working with Taiwanese and Chinese sources to buy iPod dock connector supplies in bulk, which is the only way they're normally available. He resells these in small quantities to hobbyists who want to build their own iPod accessories. Képesi quickly hooked up with Ridax, whose web support pages provided the iPod connector's pinouts and other important developer information.

Képesi put together his parts list and posted the circuit details so anyone could build the open source, dockable microphone.

Képesi sent over his design and asked if this was something that could be assembled by automation. Ridax looked it over, checked with his Chinese contacts, and said yes. After building a couple of prototypes locally, Ridax worked with the job shop in China to design and then ship the microphone.

The first order was for 1,200 pieces. Képesi and his small team kept 50 on hand and quickly sold the rest through Ridax's online storefront. The storefront took care of all fulfillment details, including shipping. Within the first few months, they'd sold more than 1,000 microphones for €29 ($46) each. To give some perspective, this price is similar to those for Belkin and MicroMemo microphones in the United States, but in Europe these products sell for about €80. Képesi and his team were selling their microphone for less than half the going rate.

While Képesi worked on the microphone, hackers Eok (in Germany) and Vinson (in France) worked on the iPod's VoIP software. Vinson was the author of a VoIP system for the Nintendo, based on the

Session Initiation Protocol (SIP).

As Vinson didn't actually own an iPod Touch, he developed the software "blind." He compiled his versions and sent them over to Eok for testing.

Before long, the team was able to get basic SIP sessions going and Vinson managed to connect the SIP software into the iPod Touch's low-level audio system. That's when the microphone and the software came together.

By New Year's 2008 you could buy a microphone, download the new Siphon software, and make and receive phone calls by setting up an account with Asterisk or with a VoIP provider like FreeCall or SIPphone's Gizmo5.

In February 2008, the team decided to split. Vinson wanted to focus on the Siphon software, commercializing it with a French VoIP company. Képesi and Eok committed themselves to further developing the TouchMods project (touchmods.net), focusing on open source hardware and software development for the iPod Touch. After this hugely successful collaboration, they agreed it was time to move on to pursue their specific interests.

» For more information: touchmods.org

» TouchMods useful links: touchmods.wordpress.com/useful-links

» Want to buy your microphone without building it from scratch? Visit Ridax at home.swipnet.se/ridax/touchmic.htm. You can also order dock connector supplies if you're looking to build your own iPod accessories.

» If you read German, there's a good interview with the development team at *Die Welt*: makezine.com/go/diewelt

Erica Sadun has written, co-written, and contributed to almost 30 books about technology, particularly in the areas of programming, digital video, and digital photography.

Soft Drink Recycling
The bottom of a soft drink or beer can makes a dandy mixing container for small batches of epoxy or other noxious concoctions.   —Frank Joy

Go-Karts Race to College

Winner gets a $10,000 college scholarship. Loser goes home.

By Nate Bell

Some high school students deliver newspapers or wash dishes to save money for college. The teens on the reality-based TV show *Design Squad* try to outbuild each other.

On our final episode of Season 2 we divided our young cast into two teams, and gave them identical sets of parts for off-road go-karts: front and rear suspension, steering, engine and rear drive train, seats, seat belts, and brakes. The teams had to design the chassis, roll cage, and side impact protection, taking into consideration how their designs would affect handling and vehicle weight.

Purple Team took a modular, design-as-you-go approach, thinking about the chassis, roll cage, and side impact protection separately. They focused on a machine that was easy to get in and out of, because the racers had to stop and pick up flags along the course.

Green Team designed the chassis, roll cage, and side impact protection as an integrated unit. This meant that Green used much less metal and kept the weight low — but they had to be careful with the design to ensure that the overall structure would be strong enough to survive intense off-road battering. Green's racing crew members were smaller and more willing to bump shoulders during the race, so

Photography by Helen Tsai

DIY TEAMWORK: (clockwise from top left) With only three days to design and build an off-road go-kart, a Purple Team member races against the clock to make a component. A Green Team member welds together their kart's frame. Green Team makes last-minute mods on race day. Purple's riders were bigger than Green's, so their kart was designed wider and with a longer wheelbase, which turned out to be a mistake.

Green designed a narrower chassis than Purple, which further reduced the kart's weight. (Any guesses yet as to which team was making better design decisions?)

The teams also considered the wheelbase design. Maneuverability would be key in an off-road course. Purple chose a longer wheelbase because of the improved ergonomics for taller racers. Green chose a shorter wheelbase, which allowed for tighter turns, and which gave them better ground clearance on the bump-ridden course.

On race day, it became clear that Green's shorter wheelbase, narrower chassis, and lighter weight resulted in a nimble off-road racer. Purple's longer wheelbase made it more difficult to complete tight turns for quick maneuvers, and their heavier kart took longer to get back to full speed after slowing down for a turn. With all of these factors playing into the outcome of the race, it's no surprise Green crossed the finish line first.

📹 For videos of the go-kart competition, visit pbskids.org/designsquad.

Nate Bell is the host of PBS's *Design Squad*.

Breezing Through Oshkosh

A maker's look at the Experimental Aircraft Association's AirVenture show. By William Gurstelle

O f all the projects that makers can conceive, I'd wager that none is so challenging to both mind and body or has such a rich and historic legacy as the home-built flying machine.

Long before the Wright Brothers, makers were trying to emulate bird flight in balloons and gliders. Early success stories were few and far between. But since the Wrights, building airplanes has been the maker's mark, the cynosure of amateur craftsmanship and mechanical design. No other amateur construction commands the respect and admiration of an airplane.

Serving the needs of skyward-dreaming makers

is the Experimental Aircraft Association (EAA), an international organization of aviation enthusiasts. Each summer, 170,000 people attend the group's week-long AirVenture show in Oshkosh, Wis. It's a happening place, so much so that the comparatively tiny Oshkosh airport temporarily becomes the world's busiest, its control tower managing hundreds of takeoffs and landings hourly.

A few of those takeoffs and landings involve the U.S. Air Force's best and most modern craft — for example, the Lockheed Martin F-22 Raptor. On demonstration flights, these airplanes scream by, 90 feet above the runway. Then, with afterburners

Photography by William Gurstelle (this page and next, top)

on, the Raptors climb vertically until the red glow of the exhaust is just a dot. It's mighty impressive in a loud, showy sort of way. But it's not inspirational in a maker sort of way. Each F-22 is the result of a million hours of highly specialized labor, and it's far more a symbol of national and global politics than an expression of technological joy.

Fortunately for makers, there's excitement and vibrancy at the other end of the runway. Far, far away from the gray-black military jets sits the airplane I liked best. It's called the Breezy.

Comparing a Breezy to an F-22 is like comparing Seabiscuit to a donkey. They both have four legs and a tail, but the differences overwhelm the similarities. I found the F-22 moderately interesting, the Breezy sublime. The Breezy is approachable, human-scaled, and, for a machine, downright cute. Given the time and inclination, any maker with enough gumption and money could probably build one.

The Breezy was conceived in 1965 by amateur aviators Charles Roloff, Carl Unger, and Bob Liposky. It remains one of the most distinctive and unusual home-built airplane designs ever imagined. And with its open cockpit, it's as close to riding a flying carpet as you're going to get.

At the Oshkosh air show, pilot Arnie Zimmerman offered me a chance to ride in his Breezy and I jumped on it. We taxied onto the concrete, one of a dozen aircraft queued up for clearance to take off. Preceding us were a formation of World War II fighter planes, a Ford Tri-Motor, and a number of conventional private aircraft.

We turned into the wind and accelerated down the runway. Within a few hundred feet, we were airborne. The airplane gained altitude fairly rapidly. I quickly found out how it feels to be 1,200 feet up with nothing holding me in but my seatbelt. Three inches of nylon strap never seemed so inadequate. At first terrified, I eventually got used to the feeling and the freedom. There's nothing between the flyer and the sky except a pair of goggles. For a view and fresh air, the open cockpit that makes a Breezy so breezy — no door, no windshield — cannot be surpassed.

In every respect, the Breezy is a real airplane, not a mere ultralight. An ultralight aircraft is defined by federal government regulations as a single-seat flying machine with a fuel capacity of 5 gallons or less, an empty weight of less than 254 pounds and a top speed of 55 knots. The Breezy's specifications exceed every ultralight limit by a factor of two or more.

FLYING HIGH: The Breezy (opposite) is as close to a flying carpet as you're going to get. Arnie Zimmerman pilots the Breezy (top). Some 170,000 visitors attend the EAA show in Oshkosh, Wis. each year (bottom).

I quickly found out how it feels to be 1,200 feet up with nothing holding me in but my seatbelt.

As homebuilt aircraft go, the Breezy is pretty simple. Its fuselage is a matrix of triangles welded from 4130 chrome-moly steel that resembles a slightly bent construction crane boom. The control surfaces are simple as well, just a rudder and a pair of elevators controlled by an exposed wire-and-pulley mechanism. (More sophisticated airplanes have additional control surfaces such as ailerons

A MAKER'S DILEMMA: Which Airplane Project Is Right for You?

Choosing between the F-22 Raptor (left) and the Breezy RLU-1 (right).

AIRCRAFT	F-22 RAPTOR	BREEZY RLU-1
LENGTH	62'1"	22'6"
CAPACITY	1 person	3 people
COST	$142 million	$100 for plans, $15,000–$17,000 for build
WINGSPAN	44'6"	33'
WEIGHT	43,340lbs	698lbs
ENGINE	2 Pratt & Whitney 35,000lb-thrust turbofans	90-horsepower, 4-cylinder reciprocating
MAXIMUM SPEED	Mach 2.42 (1,600mph)	Mach 0.11 (85mph)
SERVICE CEILING	60,000'	5,000'
ARMAMENT	M61A2 Vulcan Gatling guns, fire rate of 110 rounds/second	Depends on what the pilot is packing

When deciding between the two, there are many considerations to weigh. Sure, there's something appealing about flying a Mach 2.4 airplane with a machine gun that fires 6,600 rounds a minute. But you can buy full plans for the Breezy for about $100, while the cost of the F-22 is somewhat greater. And, the Breezy can fly more people at once.

Consensus choice: the Breezy.

and flaps.) Wings are typically bought ready-made, and the Breezy's flight characteristics are such that many different types of wings work.

Where do the wings come from? Well, sometimes they're salvaged from crashed planes, although that's just one source among many. And that's not something I choose to think about, especially when I'm 2,000 feet up with nothing to cushion me against the onrushing terrain except the hair on the head of the pilot in front of me. I checked the FAA records of crashes in this type of airplane, and I found five incidents, three of them involving fatalities. Although a thousand plans for these homebuilt planes have been sold since 1965 and thousands of flight hours logged, those numbers indicate that Breezy owners have at least a bit of the daredevil in them.

» Breezy Kits: aircraftspruce.com/catalog/kitspages/breezy.php

■ YouTube has videos showing the Breezy in flight.

William Gurstelle is a contributing editor at MAKE and the author of several books, including *Whoosh, Boom, Splat* and *Backyard Ballistics*. He lives in Minneapolis.

Photography by Getty Images (left) and Edy Shuetz (right)

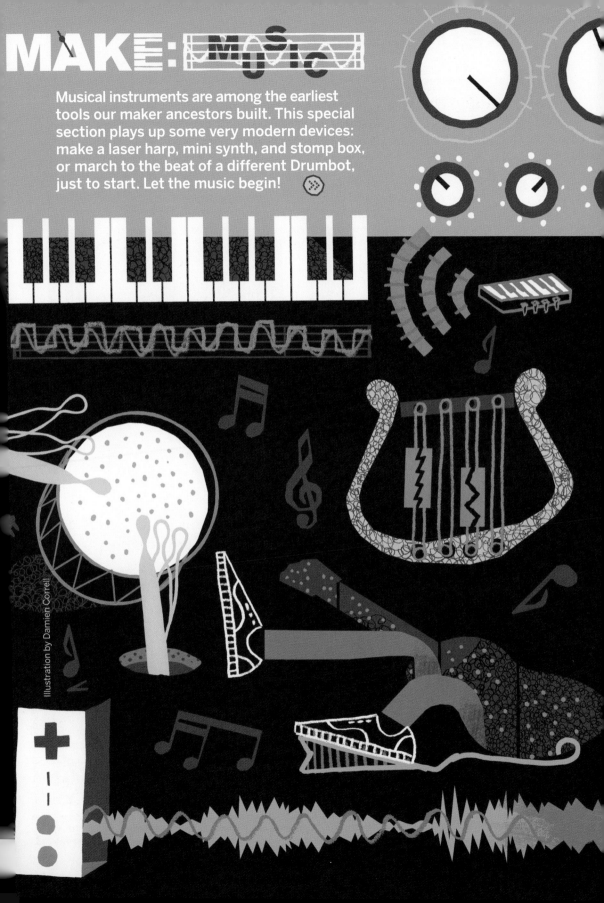

MAKE: MUSIC

Musical instruments are among the earliest tools our maker ancestors built. This special section plays up some very modern devices: make a laser harp, mini synth, and stomp box, or march to the beat of a different Drumbot, just to start. Let the music begin!

Illustration by Damien Correll

MAKE: MUSIC

Juke Box Zero

The Guitar Zeros turn plastic and programming into real hard rock.
By Jay Laney

ROCKING THE *GUITAR HERO 3* GIBSON LES PAUL!

ROCKING THE *GUITAR HERO 2* GIBSON X-PLORER!

The Guitar Zeros flex their frets for MAKE "in the key of yellow." Bass controllerist Alex Oliver, guitar controllerist Owen Grace, drummer Christian Marenbach, and singer Ryan Yount.

Live in concert at Union Hall in Brooklyn, N.Y.

Your first time at a Guitar Zeros concert can be a confusing experience. Initially, everything is fine. There's a band on the stage. They're doing their thing. They're rocking out. It's all good.

Then you notice it: the two guitarists are not actually holding guitars. The things in their hands are guitar-shaped, but they are most certainly not real guitars.

The Zeros, true to their name, are using controllers from the video game *Guitar Hero*, but they're not playing a video game. They're playing their own songs. The controller substitutes an actual guitar's range of frets and strings with just five "fret buttons" and a "strum bar." In the game, the player uses the controller to "play" a variety of hard rock covers. The Zeros play it for real.

Zeros founder Owen Grace decided that using the controller to create original material was the inspiration he and his would-be bandmates had been waiting for. Grace and the other three members, Ryan Yount, Christian Marenbach, and Alex Oliver, had wanted to start a band together. With the exception of Yount, they were all experienced musicians; this time, they wanted to experiment.

Though they played their first gig together about three weeks after Grace presented the idea, getting the controllers to do as they asked wasn't easy. Ditching *Guitar Hero* the game meant that there was no software to turn their button-mashing on the controller into actual sounds. In grad school, Grace had learned to use a musical programming environment called Max/MSP. With Max/MSP as their audio synthesizer, he developed the software that would drive the *Guitar Hero* controllers.

"It took two months for the initial round of development, followed by six months of refinement to get what we use now. Honestly, if I hadn't already known how to use Max/MSP, we may not have done this," admits Grace.

Watching the Zeros practice is almost like watching any other band: they play their songs, then everyone tells the bassist what he's doing wrong. That's where the similarity ends, though.

The high degree of control they have over the software running their instruments allows for some interesting sonic opportunities. "In our early practices, Christian or I would say, 'It'd be cool if you could do this.' Owen would show up to the next practice with whatever we were talking about already implemented," recalls Oliver.

"I think we take ourselves less seriously than most bands, and yet manage to be more focused at the same time," says Yount, the Zeros' lead singer. This may be because of the group's DIY origins, or it could be a natural result of the personalities involved. Either way, their garage-geek vibe is a large part of what makes the band unique.

The Guitar Zeros released their first EP, *Hotbird*, in November 2007. In the spirit of "making a great tool, but wanting to focus on making good music through that," Grace is giving away the software that powers the controllers, which he named Fretbuzz, on the band's website, and directions on how to convert your *Guitar Hero* controller can be found on the next page.

➕ theguitarzeros.com

Jay Laney makes manic savoir-faire seem almost effortless. He lives and works in San Francisco.

Photography by Sam Murphy

Make: **55**

21st-Century Keytars

Make your own music with *Guitar Hero* controllers.
By Owen Grace

The author unleashes "plastic bundles of star power."

It's all fun and games until someone turns those plastic *Guitar Hero* axes into real instruments. What musical possibilities lie hidden beneath those five rainbow-colored buttons?

Within a few years of the video game's launch in 2005, millions of its guitar-shaped controllers were manufactured. Sadly, many are collecting dust in closets across the globe. In my closet was one such controller, leaning awkwardly between some dirty hiking boots and a deflated soccer ball. In 2007, I pondered the depressing fate of this plastic bundle of star power. I sensed untapped potential, and I noticed how my acoustic guitar got plenty of my attention, unlike my sad old controller. What if the *Guitar Hero* controller could make music?

I knew it was possible and I saw a means to make it happen. After months of programming, I successfully repurposed the controller as a musical instrument. No hardware modifications were made — it all happens with software running on my laptop. I formed a band with friends, called the Guitar Zeros. We've got a singer and a drummer, and the other two of us use *Guitar Hero* controllers — one for guitar sounds and one for bass.

Here's how to make music with your own *Guitar Hero* controller using the software I designed.

Read about Owen Grace and the Guitar Zeros in the profile on page 54.

Photograph by Sam Murphy

After downloading and installing Fretbuzz, you're ready to make some noise. Turn the audio on and rock out! There are a bunch of different sounds: some modeled after real guitars, some more bass-like, and some more synthesizery. There's even a mode that sounds like the *Star Wars* lightsaber. Look out, Darth Vader.

Read the instructions within the software to change sound modes and learn how to use them.

SHOUT OUT: Fretbuzz was written within a unique programming environment called Max/MSP. I have to give big thanks to the makers of Max/MSP because without it, I wouldn't have known where to begin!

1. Connect your controller and computer.

A Windows PC or Mac will work, but these first few steps outline the process using a PC laptop running Windows XP.

1a. Connect the *Guitar Hero* controller to your computer. A controller with a USB connector is easiest — no adapter necessary (Figure A, next page). Otherwise, see our website for a list of adapters available for $10 to $20.

1b. Your computer may automatically detect the new USB device and download the necessary driver from the internet. Alternatively, your adapter may have come with its own driver. To be sure the controller is properly connected to your computer, go to Settings ⇒ Control Panel ⇒ Game Controllers. You should see your game controller devices listed (Figure B).

1c. Double-click the appropriate entry in the list, and you'll probably see a joystick calibration menu, much like the one in Figure C. You might not need to calibrate your *Guitar Hero* controller here, but you'll want to test all the inputs and watch the indicators light up as you press the buttons and flip the strum bar. If you're using a PlayStation 2 controller, the whammy bar may or may not be detected by your computer, depending on your adapter. Don't be discouraged — whammy bars are just for show-offs anyway, right?

2. Download Fretbuzz software.

Download the software that makes your controller and computer sing. All the components you need, and installation instructions, are free at our site.

3. Explore the musical possibilities.

The *Guitar Hero* controller has 5 fret buttons, a strum bar that can be pressed up or down, start/select buttons, and the Star Power tilt sensor inside the controller. I wanted to push the musical possibilities to the max. After months of trial and error, I developed and refined Fretbuzz. Here's a brief explanation of how it works.

Fret buttons Do 5 buttons mean you can only make 5 notes? Hardly. There are 32 different combinations of those 5 buttons, which could theoretically be assigned to 32 different notes! However, holding down all 5 at once is almost impossible to do with 4 fingers, and some combinations would require you to stretch your hand to press both the first and last buttons. Tricky.

Thus, I chose to use only the first 4 buttons for selecting notes, saving the last (orange) button for special purposes. Figure D shows all the different combinations of the first 4 buttons and how I assigned them to chords within a key.

Notice that chords are assigned in a binary progression? Pretty geeky, but it works! There are 16 different combinations, spanning 2 octaves. That's just enough of a range to work with, in my opinion.

Strum bar The strum bar is naturally used to trigger notes. Lucky for us, the bar can be pressed either up or down, enabling 2 different potential results. With the power chord guitar sound, for example, I wanted a down-strum motion to produce a palm-muted effect, while the up-strum would let the chord ring out. And if you flip the strum bar up and down rapidly, then all the chords are palm-muted.

On the other hand, with most of the bass sounds,

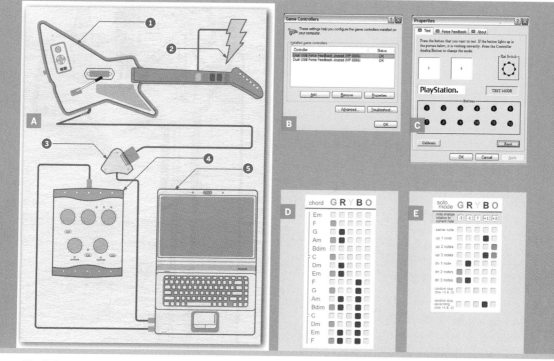

Fig. A: Connect your *Guitar Hero* axe to your computer. 1) *Guitar Hero* controller. 2) A little finger-fret skill is necessary to truly rock. 3) Controller-to-USB adapter, if needed. 4) Optional external sound card. 5) Laptop or desktop computer. Figs. B and C: Test your controller. Fig. D: Chord fingerings in Fretbuzz

the up-strum plays a note 4 steps higher, which makes it easy to play bass lines that alternate between a note and its relative fifth, common in some styles of music.

Start and select buttons Use these buttons in conjunction with the fret buttons to choose different sound modes, adjust output volume, and perform key changes on the fly.

Whammy bar On a real electric guitar, the whammy bar reduces string tension, lowering the frequencies of the notes being played. So I thought to do the same with Fretbuzz. However, not all methods of sound synthesis allow for pitch changes on the fly, so the effect is available only for certain sounds.

Tilt sensor This is where the controller gets interesting! The tilt sensor in the newer controllers is a high-quality accelerometer that detects the orientation of the guitar in 2 dimensions.

What in the world should this do, musically? There's no such tilt detector in a real guitar, so this is new terrain. I chose to apply 1 dimension of tilt to a band-pass filter, which produces a wah-pedal effect. It's good for performing solos — just ask Jimi Hendrix. What to do about the second dimension? I've tried a few different things, but I'm still exploring.

4. Try out the solo modes.

In addition to the fret combination approach for chords (Figure D), I designed 3 different solo modes that employ the fret buttons and strum bar in different ways. Imagine assigning each fret button to a relative change in pitch rather than an absolute pitch (see Figure E). In the basic solo mode, you can ascend a scale 1 note at a time by simply holding the blue fret button and flipping the strum bar. Or descend the scale by thirds by holding green.

By alternating between ascending and descending within a key, while flipping that strum bar as fast as you can, you can produce some scorching lead lines.

Any Eddie Van Halen fans out there? This guy is a two-hand-tapping master, and Fretbuzz definitely

Illustration by Julian Honoré/p4rse.com

using only the first 4 buttons. Fig. E: Solo mode in Fretbuzz. Fig. F: Use your elbow on the strum bar while using two-hand-tapping mode!

Fig. G: Engage Star Power to switch between solo and chord modes. Get ready for rock-and-roll awesomeness!

needs a two-hand-tapping mode. Much as in the basic solo mode, the fret buttons are assigned to pitches relative to one another, and the strum bar is used creatively to shift the notes of all the fret buttons at once in full-on arpeggio glory. But how do you use the strum bar when both of your hands are mashing fret buttons? With your elbow, of course (Figure F).

The concept of Star Power is unique to the *Guitar Hero* game, but I wanted to bring new meaning to it within Fretbuzz. I designed a special chord/solo combo mode where you have to engage Star Power (tilt the controller straight up) to initiate the solo playing style, then tilt the controller back down again to return to chord mode (Figure G).

5. Finally, make music.

It's up to you to use Fretbuzz however you like, but I suggest you find a friend, plug 2 controllers into your computer at once (assign 1 to the bass sounds and 1 to the guitar sounds), jam out together, and write some tunes. Then of course, turn the volume up to 11 and blast your eardrums. Only kidding.

Seriously though, it's difficult trying to re-create songs that were originally written on a real guitar. It's like learning a piece of music on guitar that was originally written for piano: sometimes shortcuts and adjustments are necessary. Fretbuzz might turn the *Guitar Hero* controller into an instrument, but it doesn't turn it into a guitar exactly.

Designing Fretbuzz has been so exciting for me. It was no trivial task to turn the *Guitar Hero* controller into a playable, dynamic, and expressive instrument. Whatever your talents and interests may be, working within a constrained medium, as I did with this project, is a super way to get your creative juices flowing.

If you have questions about this project or need help getting Fretbuzz to work on your computer, or even if this project inspired you in some totally different way and you want to bounce ideas off someone, shoot me an email (owen@theguitarzeros. com). I'd love to hear from you. Happy shredding!

Photography by Owen Grace

Drumbot Activate!

This MIDI kit just wants to bang on the drum all day. By Michael Una

It's no Buddy Rich, but this little 'bot can really lick the skins.

I used to have a drum kit in high school, and I spent hours whapping away at it in an attempt to build up some decent chops. Then I realized I wanted to do more with my hands than just play drums, so I sold my kit and bought a drum machine.

Digital drum machines can be easily programmed to play many different sounds and rhythms, but ultimately they sound a little canned. Why not make a machine that plays real drums?

My Drumbot has the programmable flexibility and sequenced tight rhythm of a drum machine, while producing a more natural sound by striking actual drums (or boxes, or tabletops, or whatever).

Building your own drum-playing robot is now affordable and easy, mostly due to advancements in programmable microcontrollers and the shared

knowledge of user communities. There are a few kits out there that'll do the job, but we'll be using Highly Liquid's MSA-R MIDI decoder kit. I enjoy this kit for its ease of assembly, low price, and solid operation.

The decoder we'll assemble will take incoming MIDI note data and translate it to control the opening and closing of 8 switches. Because the kit is preprogrammed and does all the heavy lifting, all we need to do is solder it together and attach a few switch-activated mechanical strikers to serve as our drummer's hands.

Photograph by Sam Murphy

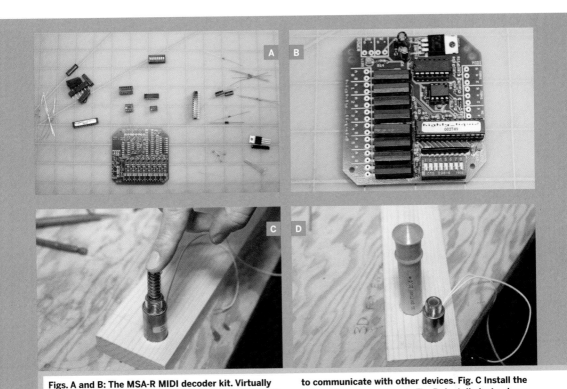

Figs. A and B: The MSA-R MIDI decoder kit. Virtually every drum machine or software sequencer uses MIDI to communicate with other devices. Fig. C Install the solenoid on a wood block. Fig. D: Install pivot column.

1. Assemble the MIDI decoder kit.

As with any project requiring soldering, make sure you've got decent ventilation and goggles for eye protection.

Take a look at all the kit components (Figure A).

Photography by Ed Troxell

MATERIALS

Highly Liquid MSA-R MIDI decoder kit
  $48 from highlyliquid.com
Dual-lead wire, about 4' **I use thin speaker wire.**
12V solenoids or small motors **around $2 each**
9V DC power supply or 9V battery
Paper clips
Wooden dowel
Pipe strapping, duct tape, or zip ties (optional)
MIDI jack

TOOLS

Device that generates MIDI signals
  such as a MIDI keyboard, sequencer, or computer
Soldering iron and solder
Needlenose pliers
Hot glue gun and glue
Drill or Dremel rotary tool (optional)
Safety glasses

Each part has a labeled place on the printed circuit board (PCB) where it'll need to be soldered in. The many-legged integrated circuits (ICs) will fit into sockets that get soldered in place, so you won't have to worry about applying too much heat to them.

TIP: It's always a good idea to expose your components to as little heat as possible — if you're having trouble with one, take a breather and come back to it later.

One more basic soldering rule: Touch your iron to the joint, then apply a small amount of solder. If you do it right, the solder will flow into the cracks and make a very nice joint. Too much solder, or improperly applied solder, will cause all sorts of headaches down the road, so it's best to do it right from the beginning.

At makezine.com/go/msaassembly you'll find the assembly notes that'll guide you through the part placement for the kit. Once each part is soldered in, trim the remaining leads to keep them from touching each other. It'll take an average-skilled solderer about 1½ hours to assemble the kit.

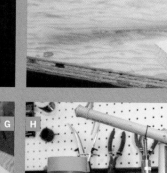

Figs. E and F: Finishing up the solenoid-powered drumstick. Mount it to the pivot stick, directly above the solenoid, then secure it to the solenoid.

Fig G: You can make drums with a plastic tube, a balloon, and some tape. Fig. H: Feel free to display the MIDI decoder kit as part of your Drumbot system.

NOTE: Some parts will only work if oriented properly, so make sure they're pointing the right way before you solder them in.

2. Attach power supply and your MIDI device.

Once the pieces are in place, attach your battery or power supply. The LEDs will light up and the power LED will remain lit. If it doesn't seem to power up, check all your solder joints and fix any that are loose or have bridged together.

Next, attach a MIDI cable to connect your MIDI-generating device to the kit. Set your device to send a continuous stream of MIDI notes, then take a look at the MSA-R firmware documentation (PDF at makezine.com/go/msafirmware) and set the DIP switch so that it's "looking for" the range of notes your MIDI device is sending.

The MSA-R kit will only "see" a range of 8 consecutive MIDI notes, so you'll have to make sure communications between the kit and your device are happening in the same note range. Once you get the 2 devices set to the same note range, you

should be able to see the LED nearest the kit's MIDI jack blinking with every message sent. Neat!

3. Build the drum strikers.

Here's where the fun begins. As the kit receives a MIDI note on/off signal, it opens and closes the 8 relay switches. All we have to do it attach ready-to-go electric motors or solenoids, and it'll fire those off in sequence.

DC motors work well with this kit, but the real drumming action will come from solenoids. A solenoid (Figure C, previous page) can be thought of as a linear DC motor — rather than rotating a central shaft, solenoids use an electromagnetic field to propel the shaft outward. Most have a spring attached that reloads the shaft after each propulsion. They're perfectly suited for tapping/striking actions.

A simple way to employ solenoids is to prop them up such that they tap on a hard surface. Cardboard, wood, and plastics all make different sounds when struck, and drumheads sound even better. However, if you want louder and more powerful strikes, you'll want to construct a lever system that will use the

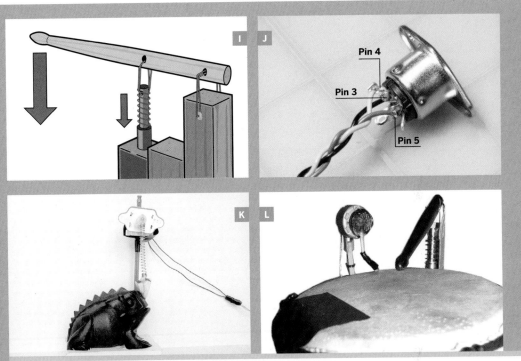

Fig. I: When current is applied to the solenoid, the drumstick is pulled down. Fig. J: MIDI jack pins 4 and 5 transmit data to the Drumbot, pin 3 is for chaining multiple devices. Fig. K: A rotary motor spins a striker to play this woodblock. Fig. L: A solenoid and rotary motor play this drum.

Illustration by Tim Lillis; photography by Michael Una

solenoid's motion to accelerate a drumstick, as shown in Figures D-I.

I was able to construct a few different levered strikers from some spare dowels and K'nex parts I had lying around. Paper clips and hot glue have held it all together pretty well, and I used some pipe strapping to attach it to the drum; you could also use duct tape or zip ties. I also have a few solenoids striking the drumhead directly, for accent notes and short rolls. This is your chance to be creative and come up with mechanisms that reveal the motion of the solenoid. Check out automata websites like dugnorth.com to find examples of simple linkages that will give a whimsical flair to your Drumbot.

A little wooden striker (cut from the end of a paint-brush) attached to a spring makes a satisfying clack on my frog-shaped woodblock (Figure K). Attached to a DC motor, the striker spins once and whacks the frog on the nose with each MIDI note sent.

4. Program your Drumbot and watch it beat time.

Once you've got your mechanical strikers in place,

take the controls of your MIDI sequencer and play around with different rhythms and beats. The devices won't ever get tired, and you'll find they can accurately tap out rhythms upward of 200 beats per minute. (Now might be the time to start that speed metal band you've been procrastinating about.)

I use my Drumbot to replace the drum machine in my live shows and the audience loves it — the sound and the sight of a robot drummer are vastly superior to a lil' grey box blinking in the corner.

The possibilities from here are endless. With 8 switches, you can control 8 low-voltage DC devices rhythmically in all sorts of configurations. Circuit-bent devices, kinetic toys, and things that light up can all be linked and sequenced into a sound-and-light show that'll impress onlookers with your ingenuity and resourcefulness. And it's fun!

Una's Drumbot in action: vimeo.com/926853

Michael Una is an audiovisual artist working and living in Chicago. His live shows and installations can been seen in the United States and abroad. una-love.com

Laser Harp

Play strings of light, using laser pointers, rangefinders, photo-cells, and Arduino.
By Stephen Hobley

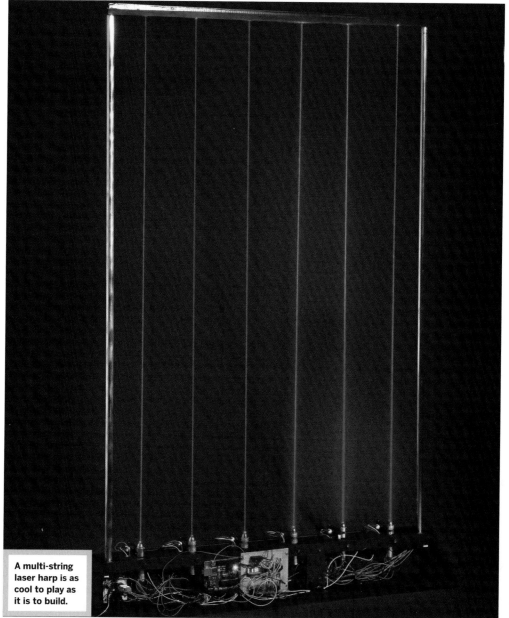

A multi-string laser harp is as cool to play as it is to build.

Photograph by Stephen Hobley

Photograph by Jacques De Selliers

One of my most vivid concert memories is seeing Jean Michel Jarre perform in 1986 at the city of Houston's 150th birthday celebration. He played music by breaking laser beams with his hands. The beams came out of the stage and went off into space, and for a long time I thought it was a fake — I couldn't understand how this instrument could work without any sensors above. That started me researching and tinkering, and 22 years later, I figured it all out and built my own.

Now I have several versions of the laser harp. The one I perform with uses a powerful laser and a scanning mirror system, designed for professional lighting effects, that splits one beam into multiple beams that can fan out and move dramatically. This article describes a simpler harp I designed more recently, which uses inexpensive laser pointers and doesn't need the scanner.

The harp works as a MIDI controller, so it doesn't make sound itself, but generates a stream of MIDI data to drive an audio synthesizer. Each beam strikes a photocell, and when the player's hand interrupts it, the sensor prompts an Arduino microcontroller to send a MIDI "Note On" message. Additionally, a range sensor reads the position of the hand, which spawns MIDI controller messages that change the sound's qualities.

First I'll show how to make a single-beam laser theremin, which changes pitch with the position of your hand. Then we'll replicate the circuit and reprogram the Arduino to produce a multi-string harp, with each beam corresponding to a different note. The Arduino has 6 analog inputs, so this harp is limited to 6 beams, but at the end of the article I'll suggest ways to expand it.

MATERIALS

Arduino board I used an Arduino Diecimila, available from the Maker Shed (makershed.com) and SparkFun (sparkfun.com). Also consider the breadboard-pluggable Boarduino from Adafruit Technologies (adafruit.com).

Laser pointers (6) any color, but they need to have a decent IR filter to avoid confusing the range sensor. I bought 25 red pointers from eBay, where prices go as low as $1 each. Green is more visible and thus scores a higher coolness factor.

DC power source, switched, 8V–12V, 2–3 amps I used an old 8.5V camcorder charger.

Adjustable voltage regulator Trossen Robotics #P-VR-DE-SWADJ, trossenrobotics.com

7805 voltage regulator, 5V from RadioShack

LM324 quad op-amp chips (2) RadioShack #276-1711

Red LEDs (6) I used a 10-LED bar array, Jameco #1553686 (jameco.com).

Resistors, ¼-watt: 220Ω (6), 1.5kΩ (6), 3.9kΩ (6), 68kΩ, 1MΩ (6)

Capacitors: 0.1µF (3) and 300µF tantalum (6)

Photocell, 100mW (6) Jameco #202403

Sharp GP2D12 or GP2D120 IR range sensors (6) from Trossen Robotics

Tumbled rocks, translucent (6) craft or bead store

Potentiometer, 100kΩ from RadioShack

5-pin DIN (MIDI) connector from RadioShack

Blank circuit boards I used 1 dual mini and 1 medium, RadioShack #276-148 and #276-168.

24-gauge hookup wire various colors

Heat-shrink tubing

8-pin headers (5) (optional)

Aluminum tubes, ½" × 36" (2)

Wood and screws I used ½" fiberboard

Black paint

TOOLS

NOTE: I've developed my projects on a PC, so the software tools I use are PC-based, but there are equivalent tools for the Mac and Unix/Linux.

Computer

MIDI utility software to test output. I recommend MIDI-OX (midiox.com).

Software synthesizer I recommend Superwave P8 (home.btconnect.com/christopherg/main.htm).

USB-MIDI interface such as M-Audio Uno

Soldering equipment and solder

Insulated wire various colors

Wire cutters and strippers

Multimeter

Alligator leads (2)

Saw

Drill

Vise and clamps

Stephen Hobley, a photographer by trade, wants to continue tinkering with electronic instruments, but lately his brand-new role as "Dad" seems to take up most of his time.

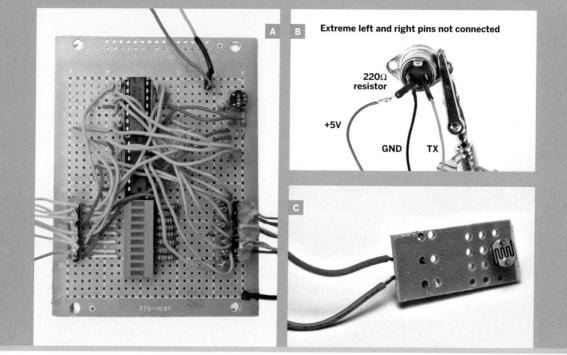

Fig. A: The detector board uses 2 quad op-amp chips to support 6 detector circuits (2 op-amps are unused).
Fig. B: MIDI jack wiring, with signal pin TX from Arduino.

Fig. C: A small piece of perf board holds the photo-detector for easy mounting.

Build the Pieces

We'll build the main electronic components first and then put them together. We'll start with the common power supply, light detector circuit board, and MIDI output jack. Then we'll add photocells, range sensors, and lasers — 1 of each for the theremin, and 6 of each for the harp.

POWER SUPPLY

I built the power supply on a mini circuit board following the schematic at makezine.com/15/laser harp. A 7805 regulator steps down the 8.5V from my camcorder charger to 5V for the range sensors. An adjustable voltage regulator lets you tune the power to the lasers to just above the detection threshold. The Arduino gets 8.5V directly, since it has its own onboard voltage regulator. To suck up any power spikes, I added a 0.1µF "bypass cap" across each of the 3 output voltages: 5V, variable, and 8.5V. These capacitors are optional. Finally, to neaten the connections out, I used two 8-pin headers for the outputs to the lasers and range sensors.

DETECTOR CIRCUITS

The photocells (aka light-dependent resistors or LDRs) are on their own little boards, across from the lasers. But I assembled the rest of the detector circuitry onto the larger circuit board (Figure A). The board needs to have 1 circuit for the theremin, or 6 circuits in parallel for the harp. Each of the two LM324 op-amp chips supports 4 detector circuits, and I went ahead and created 8 circuits, even though the harp only needs 6. The 68K and 100K resistors create a shared reference voltage, so we only need 1 of each. See the schematic online.

MIDI JACK

Wire the MIDI output jack by connecting pin 5 to the TX pin on the Arduino, pin 2 to circuit ground, and pin 4 through a 220Ω resistor to +5V. (MIDI jack pins are numbered 3, 5, 2, 4, 1, from left to right, facing the pins.) The outermost pins, 1 and 3, are not used for MIDI (Figure B).

LASERS AND PHOTOCELLS

The lasers connect in parallel to the variable voltage

Photography by Stephen Hobley

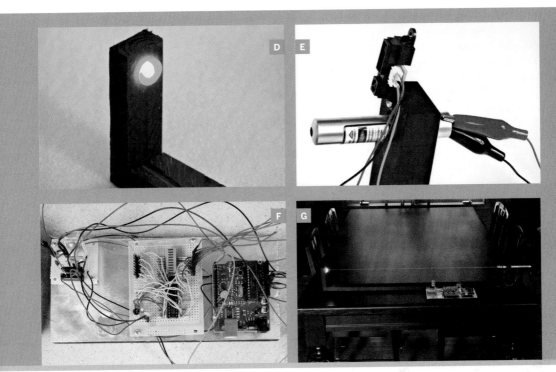

Fig. D: A tumbled translucent rock spreads laser light over the photodetector. Fig. E: The rangefinder works better when positioned vertically, away from the reflective laser pointer barrel. Fig. F: The power supply board, detector board, and Arduino on a wooden base. Fig. G: A 1-string optical theremin with green laser.

on one side and to ground on the other. I soldered the photocells to small pieces of perf board for easier mounting (Figure C). They connect in parallel to +5V on one side and to the + input pins of the op-amps on the other.

RANGE SENSORS

Anyone who has played with a touchless D-Beam control on a Roland synthesizer will recognize these sensors immediately. The GP2D12/GP2D120 range sensors fire a pulse of IR light and measure distance by triangulating on the reflection.

For musical applications, I've found that the output from these sensors can be noisy, due to the constantly flashing IR drawing a lot of current every 40ms. You can smooth the output by connecting a capacitor between voltage (pin 3) and ground (pin 2); I used some 300µF tantalum caps.

You can also filter the signal with a dedicated filter circuit (see schematic online), or in the software, by averaging consecutive readings and using the average value.

Before connecting the range sensors, I removed them from their plastic housings. They connect in parallel to +5V power, ground, and the Arduino's analog input pins 0–5.

The output from the range sensors is nonlinear, so the software converts output voltage into centimeters of distance using a simple equation, courtesy of Acroname Robotics (acroname.com). For the GP2D12 sensor:

Range [cm] = (6787 / (Voltage – 3)) – 4

And for the GP2D120:

R = (2914 / (V + 5)) – 1

Laser Theremin

Here's an optical version of a theremin, with 1 laser beam controlling both Note On/Off and pitch.

1. Download the Arduino programming software from arduino.cc. Upload the program *MAKE_MIDI_TEST.pde* from makezine.com/15/laserharp to your Arduino. This program lets the Arduino generate test MIDI messages. Set the baud rate of the Arduino to 31250.

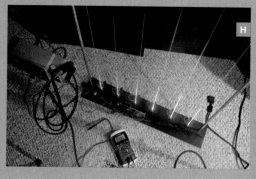

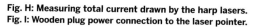

Fig. H: Measuring total current drawn by the harp lasers.
Fig. I: Wooden plug power connection to the laser pointer.

Fig. J: Author Stephen Hobley plays his full-sized laser harp, which was a huge hit at the Bay Area Maker Faire in May (see page 86).

2. Connect the MIDI jack to your computer with a USB-MIDI interface. Launch MIDI-OX (or equivalent software) and open that port. You should see Note On and Note Off messages in the MIDI inspector. If not, then test the +5V, ground, and TX pins for connectivity.

If the MIDI test is OK, upload the laser theremin program *MAKE_THEREMIN.pde* to the Arduino.

3. Take one of your laser pointers apart and measure the battery voltage. Adjust the variable regulator on your power supply board until its output matches this voltage. This lets you run the laser from your power supply board. One neat way to connect it is with alligator clips.

4. Now make the physical frame. I cut a long piece of scrap wood into 3 pieces: to make a base, a laser holder, and a detector holder.

Drill the laser holder piece for the laser to fit through horizontally, and drill a smaller perpendicular hole for a screw to hold down its power button.

5. Drill a hole through the detector holder where the laser will shine, tape the photosensor board to the outside with the sensor facing in, and glue a translucent tumbled rock over the hole in front (Figure D, previous page). The rock diffuses the light, which helps the sensor see it.

6. Next, attach the range sensor to the laser. I found that it worked better mounted vertically (Figure E) — when it was horizontal, I think the IR beam was reflecting off the laser pointer's barrel and causing misreadings. Having a rangefinder too close to a wall can also diminish accuracy.

7. Connect the photosensor circuit's output from the op-amp to pin 2 on the Arduino and connect the rangefinder's output to Analog In 0. Connect your computer back to the MIDI out and run MIDI-OX. Switch everything on (Figure G). Adjust the pot on the detector board so that the LED just comes on. At this point, breaking the laser beam with your hand should switch it off, and MIDI-OX should show you Note On, Note Off, and Pitch Bend messages as you move your hand in the beam.

That's it. Swap MIDI-OX for a soft-synth, or plug the MIDI jack into a hardware synthesizer, and you're playing!

Laser Harp

Now we'll expand on the theremin idea and create a 6-beam laser harp.

1. Build the frame. I made a wooden base to hold the lasers, rangefinders, and circuitry. Two metal tubes at either end support a top tube, which has 6 holes drilled through its underside to expose the photosensors. Space the lasers at least 4" apart, or else cross-talk between the range sensors can throw off their readings.

2. Wire the other lasers and photosensor/detector/ rangefinder loops in parallel with the first ones; see the schematic online. For neatness on the detector board, I used 8-pin headers for the photosensor and Arduino connections.

Also check that the variable regulator can handle the current drawn by the lasers: multiply the lasers' amperage by 6, and confirm that it's below the voltage regulator's rated max current. To make sure, you can also measure the current that comes into the regulator (Figure H).

3. Instead of messing with alligator clips, I made connector plugs for the laser pointers. I cut a slot in the back of each with a Dremel tool, made a wood plug to fit into the barrel, and thumbtacked a wire to each end (Figure I). Insert the plug, pass the wires through the slot, and screw on the back. The case contact in back will be ground. To keep the lasers switched on if the screws slip, wrap the barrels with electrical tape.

4. Connect the detector outputs from the op-amps to Arduino pins 2–7 and connect the range sensor outputs to the Arduino's analog input pins 0–5. Adjust the potentiometer until all 6 LEDs come on. You should now be able to turn them off individually by breaking the 6 beams. If ambient light becomes a problem, cut rings of narrow PVC pipe, paint them black, and attach one around each detector. If the lasers just miss the photosensor holes, glue on tumbled rocks as diffusers.

5. Upload the program *MAKE_HARP1_CTRL.PDE* to the Arduino, and start playing. The software assigns the MIDI note numbers 60, 62, 64, 65, 67, and 69 to the beams, but you can change this by editing the `notearray[]` structure. The controller messages from the range sensors are sent as note 74. With my synthesizer, this changes the filter sweep and creates a funky, retro synth sound.

You can also try *MAKE_HARP1_VEL.PDE*, a modified version of the code that maps your hand position to MIDI velocity, to mimic how hard you would strike a key on a keyboard.

Further Development

You're not limited to just playing notes. Ableton Live software allows you to MIDI-trigger drum loops, sequences, and other musical events. It's not free, but you can download a demo version at ableton.com.

If you want to go crazy and add more beams, you'll need to expand the digital and analog inputs of the Arduino using a multiplexer. There are a couple of neat, off-the-shelf ways to do this. I'll mention two here, and you can find more at the Arduino Playground (arduino.cc/playground).

One approach is to use an analog multiplexer like the R4 AIN MIDIbox module, which is based on the 4051 chip (kit available from AVI Showtech, avishowtech.com). This will support 32 inputs, for 32 harp strings.

With some clever programming, you should be able to bypass the detector board and read the laser harp through the analog multiplexer. To do this, connect the photocell array's outputs to the multiplexer's inputs, feed the multiplexed output to the Arduino, and detect which beams are broken in your software.

You can also use a digital multiplexer like the R5 DIN Module, another MIDIbox kit from AVI Showtech, which is based on the 74HC165 chip. With these, you can chain modules together to support an unlimited number of inputs.

If you want to tackle a full-sized scanning laser harp (Figure J), visit my website, stephenhobley.com.

➕ For project code, schematics, and further development resources, visit makezine.com/ 15/laserharp.

Acknowledgment: This project is a testament to the collaborative power of the internet. I could not have done it without the help of many people who were good enough to answer the questions I posted on a variety of forums. I'd like to take this opportunity to pass on my gratitude!

The MoofTronic Mini Synth

New sounds from a truly tiny instrument.
By Brian McNamara

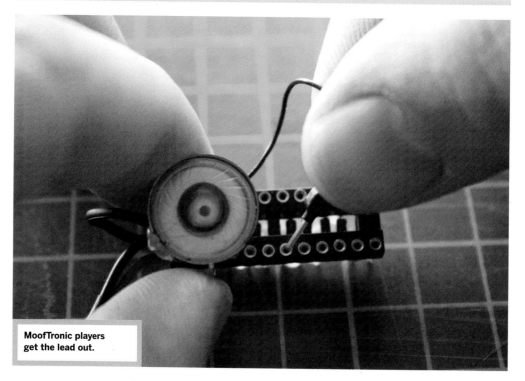

MoofTronic players get the lead out.

I was playing around with a Picaxe microcontroller one day, trying to make a little keyboard. I wanted to build an absolutely minimal hardware frame that I could put together quickly without a circuit board.

The result was the MoofTronic — a small electronic instrument built on a 24-pin IC socket. To play 8 different notes (1 octave in the key of C) against a fast-modulation drone, you touch a stylus to 8 legs of the socket. It also has a small antenna that you can touch to add an effect to the note being played. The 8-pin Picaxe microcontroller that runs the software and generates the sounds sits in one end of the socket and has a small speaker mounted on top. A programming port allows you to easily debug and test new sound-making programs.

Brian McNamara lives in a small town near Canberra, Australia. By day he works at a university designing and repairing equipment for a biological research facility; by night he designs, hacks, and bends kids' toys and musical instruments.

Photography by Brian McNamara

Fig. A: Building the 8-resistor ladder under the IC socket. Fig. B: The voltage regulator tucked underneath the socket.

1. Fit the 8 resistors to the IC socket bottom.

The 8 resistors form a ladder of increasing resistance that allows the socket pins to play different notes. Start the ladder by bending the legs of the 1K resistor around pins 12 and 13, leaving enough wire on one end to join pin 13 to pin 14. Trim excess wire and repeat down the socket, joining pin pairs with the 2.2K, 3.3K, 4.7K, 12K, 22K, 33K, and 39K resistors, in order (Figure A). No jumper is needed between pins 20 and 21. Finally, solder the resistors in place. See makezine.com/15/mooftronic for a schematic.

2. Add the voltage regulator.

Trim pin 3 of the 78L05 voltage regulator to about ⅛", then solder it to the red wire of the battery clip and cover the joint with heat-shrink tubing. With the 78L05 facing up, bend pins 1 and 2 out at right angles, pin 1 to the left and pin 2 to the right. Positioning the regulator flat within the socket, bend pin 1 around the IC socket's pin 1 and bend the regulator's pin 2 around the socket's pin 24

(Figure B). Trim the wires, but don't solder yet.

3. Wire the link and 10K resistor.

Solder a wire diagonally from pin 1 to pin 20 of the IC socket. Connect pin 22 to pin 24 with a 10K resistor. Wrap the legs around the pins, but don't solder yet.

4. Add the stylus and antenna.

To make the stylus, strip and tin a 5" length of wire and fit some heat-shrink over one end, leaving a bit of metal exposed. Solder the other end to pin 22 on the socket. For the antenna, solder some leftover wire from a resistor leg to pin 3 of the socket, and bend it around to the top (Figure C, next page).

5. Add the program port.

Cut three 4" lengths of wire and solder 1 wire each to socket pins 2, 23, and 24. Cut the wire from pin 2 in half, and solder-splice a 22K resistor in the middle. Cover the resistor with heat-shrink. Solder the wire from the 22K resistor to the ring (middle) contact of the 3.5mm audio jack, solder the pin 24

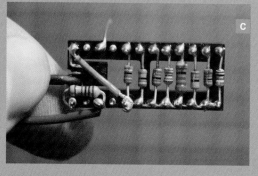

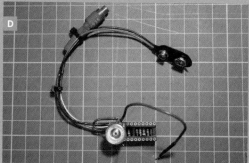

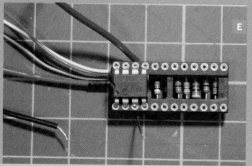

Fig. C: The socket soldered with the antenna (bare wire, top) and stylus (blue wire, lower left). Fig. D: The MoofTronic connected to the programming port. Wires are bundled together with cable ties. Fig. E: The Picaxe microprocessor fit into the socket. Fig. F: The headphone speaker glued on top of the Picaxe.

wire to the jack's tip contact, and solder the pin 23 lead to the sleeve (inner) contact.

Solder a 10K resistor between the tip and ring contacts of the audio jack, and reinforce the connections with ⅜" heat-shrink. Finally, bundle the programming port and battery clip leads together with 2 cable ties (Figure D).

6. Fit the Picaxe microcontroller.

Fit the Picaxe-08M into the 24-pin IC socket. Pin 1 on the Picaxe goes to pin 1 of the IC socket (Figure E).

NOTE: I used a 12.7mm (0.5") wide socket, so I had to bend the Picaxe pins slightly. If you use a 10.16mm (0.4") wide IC socket, you don't have to bend the IC socket pins, but it's a bit harder to fit the resistors.

7. Add the speaker.

I used an old in-ear headphone speaker, so the first thing was to disengage it from the surrounding plastic. Glue the speaker onto the Picaxe, and add a bit more glue where its delicate little wires attach to the speaker coil. Cut the speaker wires to about

1" and solder one to socket pin 24 and the other to pin 21. Solder the black (−) battery wire to socket pin 24, and reinforce the socket ends of the headphone wires with more glue (Figure F).

8. Program the microcontroller.

Download and install the Picaxe Programming Editor software, free from rev-ed.co.uk/picaxe. Then download the *mooftronic.bas* program file from makezine.com/15/mooftronic.

Connect the serial cable from the computer to the programming port on the MoofTronic (Figure G).

Launch the Picaxe Programming Editor. Select File → Open, then open the file *mooftronic.bas* from the folder you downloaded it into.

Power up the MoofTronic by connecting the 9V battery. Now load the program onto the MoofTronic by clicking Picaxe → Run (Figure H).

You'll see a dialog box with a progress bar while the program is loading. This takes only a few seconds. Then a second dialog box will tell you that you have successfully programmed the Picaxe (Figure I).

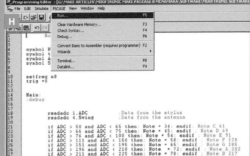
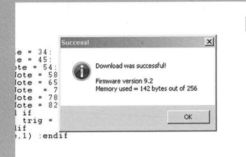

Fig. G: The MoofTronic connected to the computer via the Picaxe serial programming cable. Fig. H: Uploading the MoofTronic code to the Picaxe.

Fig. I: Program upload done. Fig. J: Protecting the connections with hot glue.

9. Test and glue.

Fit the 9V battery into the battery clip, and test that the device works. Start making noise with the MoofTronic by touching any pin from 5 to 12 of the IC socket with the stylus. If you also touch the small antenna with your finger, the pitch of the sound changes, and quickly goes up and down.

Once it's all working correctly, fill the bottom section of the IC socket with glue from the hot glue gun. This stabilizes all the little wires and keeps them from breaking off (Figure J).

10. Go nuts.

One of the best things about the MoofTronic is that the software can easily be changed, reprogrammed, and tested on the hardware in a matter of minutes. So once you've built the hardware, go crazy hacking some new sounds!

See a video of the MoofTronic in action at makezine.com/go/mooftronic.

USB Gamepad Music Controller

Make a responsive, stage-ready effects controller from a common gamepad.
By Brian Schmierer

Real musicians adjust levels and effects with serious-looking controls.

For years, I enjoyed building analog effects pedals for guitarists. Today's digital VST (Virtual Studio Technology) effects can do far more, but their interfaces are ill-suited to performing musicians. Having to hunt for a control on a laptop screen or a big piece of studio equipment ruins the mood.

This project is a small USB controller box that combines the flexibility of VSTs with the easy physicality of a pedal. Inside, it has the circuit board from a gamepad, whose fast-responding electronics lend themselves to work as music controls. You don't have to worry about resistance, capacitance, or anything like that, because the manufacturer already did all the work. Thanks, game controller engineers!

By assigning the parameters of a software effect to the box's switches and pots, you can control it immediately and intuitively during a performance. The controller has a footprint no larger than a guitar pedal, but it's 100 times more flexible: the same

device can be a simple delay or a complex synth.

It's true that you can buy something functionally similar if you want to throw down $200 at Guitar Center, but you can build this controller for just $30 or $40 over a weekend, and customize its look and control layout for your personal music and performance tastes. I've even built a wireless version.

Brian Schmierer is a multi-media artist living in San Francisco. He is the co-owner of Sound Arts (soundarts.org), a recording facility in the Mission District that specializes in experimental and traditional recording techniques.

Photography by Sam Murphy

Build the Controller

1. Start deconstructing the gamepad by unscrewing all the screws in the back. They almost always hide a screw under a sticker, so take off all stickers, warnings, and cautionary tales.

2. Open the back (Figure A, next page) and unscrew any screws that hold the PCB (printed circuit board) in place. Carefully pull the board out of the housing, along with all other parts. This board will be your best friend and your worst enemy during this project.

3. Let's get to work. Find the contact area for each button on the board, and follow its printed traces back to the button's leads (soldered contact points). Each button has 2 contact points. Draw a map or write down the locations of each pair (Figure B).

4. Now we'll replace each button with a switch by connecting it to the button's contact points. Cut 5" lengths of hookup wire, strip and tin the ends, and use the soldering iron to tack them down to the button contacts on the board. Applying solder directly to the board will probably cause a mess. The contact points are small, so it helps to have a fine tip on your soldering iron.

5. Connect the switches to the wires (Figure C). I used 3-pin (double-throw) toggle switches, soldering one wire to the middle pin and the other to either of the outside pins, but 2-pin (single-throw) switches work just as well. Either way, it helps to solder all the switches at the same time and orient them all in the same direction. Being consistent will help later if you need to troubleshoot or want to transplant the electronics into a new controller.

6. For the gamepad's Start button, follow the same procedure: follow its 2 traces to their solder points, and wire them to your momentary switch.

7. Next let's solder our potentiometers (Figure C). Each has 3 connections: 2 sides and a wiper, which is usually in the middle. Notice the orientation of the potentiometers in the controller, and follow the same order for the solder points on your potentiometers. You can test the leads with a multimeter measuring ohms or by plugging the controller into a computer and running a Max test patch available at makezine.com/15/gamepad, but do not solder the controller while it's plugged in.

8. Wire the LEDs. My WingMan gamepad had 3 LEDs, 1 constantly on when powered, and the other 2 switched back and forth by the controller's Select button. These are not necessary for your music controller's functionality, but they look cool and will help when you're playing a live gig and the light is low. I substituted my own LEDs, connecting them in the same manner as the switches: trace, test, and then solder. Again, tin the wires first and hot-tack them down rather than applying solder to the board.

9. You now have new appendages on the old brain, so plug the controller into a computer and test the new switches and pots to make sure everything still works. Also confirm that the connections are solid.

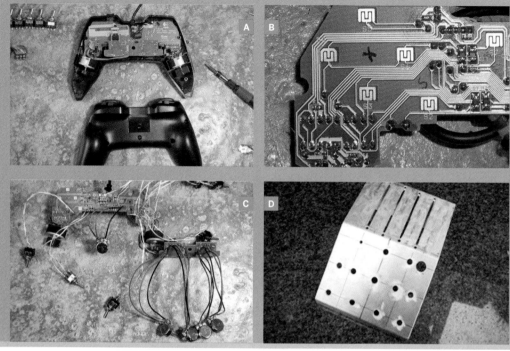

Fig. A: Back removed from gamepad. I used a Logitech WingMan RumblePad, which has an extra pot — bonus! Fig. B: Button traces and contact points on the PCB.

Fig. C: Toggle switches wired to button contacts on the board, and potentiometers wired to knob contacts. Fig. D: Slider, switch, and knob holes cut in the enclosure.

You don't want to put all the work into this thing just to drop it and have it fail.

10. If your controller has vibration (many do), cut the wires to the motors and tape them off separately with electrical tape.

11. Now for the fun part: housing this beast. This is where you can really shine and make your controller unique. Enclosures like the one I used come blank, so you need to cut holes for your components. I laid out and measured where I wanted everything, marked the box, then started to drill and cut. For the switch, knob, and LED holes, I used a graduated drill bit, and for the slider tracks I used a Dremel (Figure D). If the enclosure lacks PCB grooves, mount the board inside with screws and stand-offs.

12. If you want to paint or seal the enclosure, sand it with 600-grit sandpaper after all holes are drilled and cuts made.

13. When I make guitar pedals, I prime the enclosure

with gray Krylon primer, spray the final color, and then seal it with a clear gloss. For this controller, I painted the top black, left the sides plain brushed aluminum, and coated all parts with clear gloss.

14. Assemble the controller (Figure E), and you have it! Now all you have to do is write some badass software for it in Max.

Set Up the Software

Now that you have your controller, let's get into the software side of things. We need an application that takes the values from the switches and pots and uses them to process or produce audio. To do this, I use Max (cycling74.com), but Pure Data will also work.

Max is a patch-based application builder, which means you can use it to connect your box's outputs to VSTs and other modules the same way you would connect hardware devices, by routing from device to device with patch cords. The Max "patches" you build can process the audio themselves as stand-alone apps, or else translate incoming control signals into MIDI data to send to other applications,

Photography by Brian Schmierer

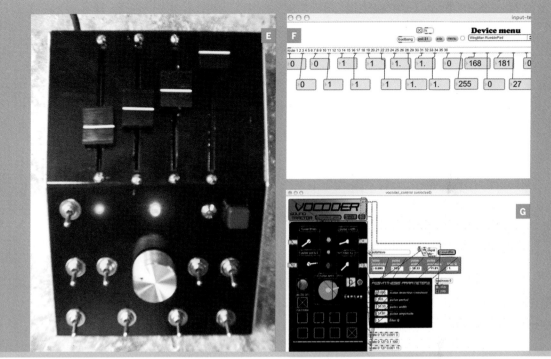

Fig. E: The finished controller. Fig. F: The Max test patch (detail) showing device inputs. Digital inputs need to be scaled from 0–255 to 0–127 for MIDI.

Fig. G: Inputs from the USB controller patched to a sample Vocoder app in Max.

like Ableton Live. If you're not familiar with Max (aka Max/MSP), I recommend running through a couple of the included tutorials before getting into the software building. For stand-alone apps, a good place to start is with the sample patches in Max's sample effects folder: Vocoder, Compressor, Reverb, and Transposer.

Whatever you do, your first job is to determine the input channels that your USB device assigns to its controllers. Run the Max test patch from makezine.com/15/gamepad, open your gamepad in the Device menu, and watch the value boxes while you flick switches and twiddle knobs. Look for the channels where the numbers change, analog (0–255) for pots and digital (0–1) for switches (Figure F). Label the inputs, and then patch each analog input to a Scale object to reduce its range to 0–127. Save the app under a new name.

As an example stand-alone app, here's how to turn your box into a Vocoder. In Max, open the folder *Applications/Examples/Effects/Classic Vocoder* and load the file *classic_vocoder.maxpat* (Figure G). Go ahead and tinker — load files, plug in a MIDI

keyboard, figure out what this thing is and how you want to use it. Associate the I/O (input/output) objects' DSP properties with your computer's microphone input and internal speakers, or other devices. Tinker with the patch in Edit mode and see how it sounds in Run mode.

To make the patch work through your gamepad effects box, copy and paste it into your saved USB inputs patch, and then connect the input channels into the vocoder parameters you want them to affect. You might want to adjust knob/slider behavior by adding or changing Scale objects.

To create a Max patch that translates control inputs into MIDI output, follow the included MIDI tutorial. Basically, you use the Control Out (ctlout) object to assign MIDI channels to outgoing messages. Keep your patch (Max application) open while it runs, and you can see the MIDI messages it generates and sends out.

I like to use the gamepad controller to send data to Ableton Live, but it can send MIDI to a soft-synth or pretty much any other music software.

Go get 'em, tiger!

Hooked on Phononics

Filter sound frequencies with an array of metal tubes.
By Charles Platt

Block audible frequencies with this series of tubes.

Few people can claim to own a phononic band-gap filter — and even if they did, they might have a hard time explaining why they need one.

Still, if you like the idea of a device that has mysterious physical properties, is the subject of numerous academic papers, and could provide a unique "wow" factor to boost your status in your power-nerd peer group, a phononic band-gap filter could be just the thing. Best of all, you can build one for well under $100 using wood, electrical conduit, and maybe a few cable ties.

Photography by Charles Platt

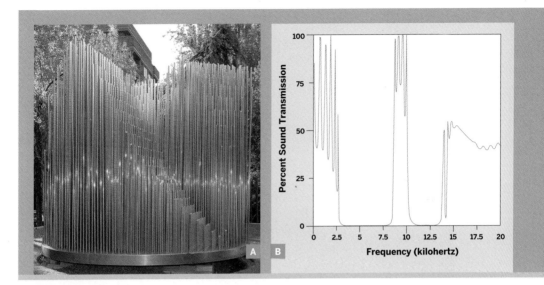

Graph B: Percent Sound Transmission vs. Frequency (kilohertz), x-axis 0 to 20, y-axis 0 to 100.

Band-Gap Filters

First let's resolve any confusion between *phononic* and *photonic*. Photonic (with a T) band-gap filters are a hot item in telecommunications research. For reasons rooted in quantum theory, if you shine light into a certain type of crystalline structure, some of the photons are blocked, even though they're smaller than the holes in the structure. The band of light frequencies emerges with a gap in it — hence the term band-gap filter.

Interestingly, the filtering effect is very scalable. It should even work the same way with ocean waves as it does with light waves, leading some scientists to propose that a pattern of concrete columns could prevent beach erosion by blocking wave motion, while still allowing tides to flow without interference.

Somewhere between the tiny wavelengths of light and the huge wavelengths of the ocean, we find vibrations that are audible and may be described as phononic (with an N). A tone of 10kHz, up near the limit of human hearing, creates waves of air pressure about 1.4" (3.5cm) apart. To build a "crystal structure" that will block such audio waves, we need nothing more sophisticated than a grid of rods.

Intuitively, it seems that all audio frequencies should pass through gaps between the rods without any problem, but theory says that they can't, and indeed they don't. This was first verified in 1995 when scientists from the Materials Science Institute of Madrid noticed that a public sculpture by Eusebio Sempere (Figure A), consisting of vertical rods about 3cm in diameter and spaced about 10cm apart, looked like a band-gap filter. Sure enough, when they

dragged some test equipment to the site, they found that some sounds were slightly attenuated.

From Lab to Hardware Store

Finding a practical application for phononic band-gap filters has been a challenge, because they must be large and made from rigid materials, which tend to be expensive. If appropriate patterns could be designed into buildings, they could permit ventilation while canceling noise, especially near highways and in industrial environments. But for our purposes, let's just see if we can make one work.

Most of the necessary info can be found in papers such as "Phononic crystal with low filling fraction and absolute acoustic band gap in the audible frequency range: A theoretical and experimental study" by Vasseur, Deymier, Khelif, et al., published in *Physical Review E*, May 2, 2002.

It's not what anyone would describe as beach reading, but buried in its text is a valuable take-home message for those of us who like to build stuff. The scientists blocked significant segments of the audio spectrum using copper tubes 28mm in diameter, spaced 2mm apart. Figure B shows a detail copied from one of their sound filtering graphs.

For less than $40 I carried home a bundle of 10 lengths of ¾" steel electrical conduit, each 10' long. For mysterious reasons known only to licensed electricians, the so-called ¾" conduit is not ¾" in diameter, on the inside or the outside. Its outside diameter is about 0.92", which I thought should be close enough to 28mm to achieve at least some filtering effect.

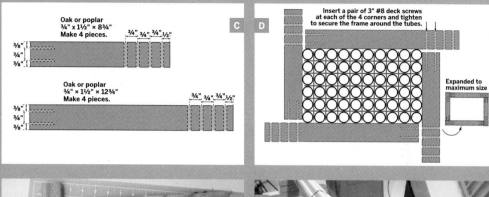

Figs. C–E: Assemble a frame to hold a bundle of conduit. For each piece, drill the 2 end holes 1½" deep with a ⅛" drill bit, and the 4 side holes with a ⁷⁄₃₂" drill

bit. Fig. F: A band saw makes swift work of cutting 10 conduits at once. Fig. G: Lengths of conduit stacked between the frames. Pieces of cable ties maintain a gap

---

The only remaining problem was how to set up a 6×10 array of tubes with a consistent and precise separation of 2mm. Here's how I tackled it.

Building a Phononic Filter

1. I sawed 6 pieces, approximately 20" in length, from each 10' length of conduit.

2. I decided to put spacers between the tubes at each end of the 6×10 array, and then clamp them with adjustable frames. For spacers I used cable ties, since they were just under 2mm thick and could be easily trimmed to fit. For the frames I used pieces of ¾"×1½" oak, cut and drilled as shown in Figure C and assembled as in Figures D and E. The advantage of this design is that it will expand to allow larger tubing spacers if you want to vary the parameters of your experiment in the future.

3. After assembling the frames loosely, I stood them opposite each other and started stacking the pieces of conduit between them, inserting spacers as I went along, as in Figure G.

4. After laying in all the conduits, I tightened the frames till they gripped securely enough for me to handle the array (Figure H).

5. Now I was ready for the audio test. Ideally this should have been done in an anechoic chamber — an insulated room in which all sound is absorbed and none reflected. Unfortunately, I don't happen to own an anechoic chamber, so I nailed together a couple of 1' square frames of 2×4 pine, stood one frame in front of my filter and the other behind it, and draped a blanket over the whole thing to make a sound-absorbing tunnel.

6. I placed a speaker from my stereo at one end of the tunnel, and the second stereo speaker outside the tunnel, so that I could use the balance control on my stereo to switch between the speakers for an A–B comparison. Then I played an audio test CD to generate a series of tones, and placed my ear to the band-gap filter.

It seemed to perform as specified, attenuating some frequencies, although of course the close-

Illustrations by Charles Platt

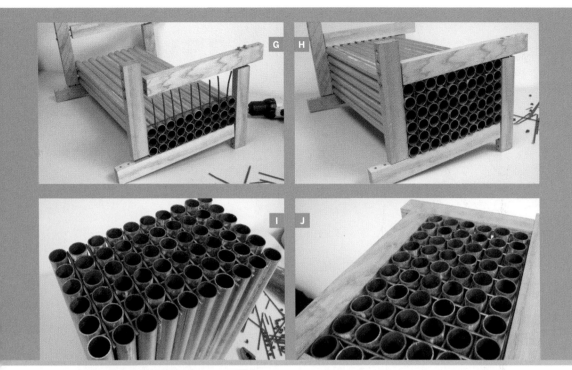

between each tube and the next. After clamping one end, it's easy to insert spacers at the other. Fig. H: The completed, clamped array. Fig. I: Wider spacers (such as copper rods) can be substituted for cable ties. Fig. J: After the wooden frame is expanded, it can be retightened around the wider-spaced conduits.

spaced grid of tubes dampened all sounds to a noticeable extent. To be really sure, I would need a sine wave generator capable of producing constant-amplitude waves from 50Hz to 20kHz, through a really good speaker, with an equally good microphone feeding into a computer sound card and audio software displaying at least 30 bands of frequencies.

7. Still, I was sufficiently intrigued to experiment further. I unscrewed one of the tube frames, removed my cable-tie spacers, and inserted new spacers made from ⅛"-diameter copper rod, as in Figure I. I expanded the frame, reattached it, and then did the same thing with the frame at the other end (Figure J). I actually seemed to get more noticeable audio effects through this configuration.

8. Lastly, I built a second filter using ½" conduit spaced 1" apart in a triangular pattern. This didn't work at all — at least not on sound waves. Possibly if I put it in a bathtub, it could block some ripples. I haven't tried this yet.

There's a serious side to all this. Anyone with minimal skills and tools can investigate a phenomenon that has exercised the abilities of scientists in heavily funded university laboratories. When Ph.D.s studying phononic band-gap phenomena start writing their next grant applications, maybe they should consider sending the work out to home hobbyists, to tap our "distributed workshop capability" — just as SETI uses distributed computer power donated by space enthusiasts who hope to discover extraterrestrial messages.

After reviewing this article, materials scientist Dr. Pierre Deymier (who coauthored the paper cited earlier) suggests that plastic tubes may work almost as well as metal tubes. Plastic tends to flex, which would affect the tubing gaps, but large-diameter PVC pipes should be sufficiently rigid while blocking a lower frequency range. Maybe a phononic filter fabricated from 5" sewer pipes? Time for a new experiment!

Charles Platt is a section editor for MAKE

Stomp Box Basics:
Tremolo and Fuzz

Simple guitar effects circuits you can build. By Charles Platt

STOMP BOX 1.0: Harry DeArmond's electromechanical tremolo generator, well over 50 years old.

Back in the day when guitar players marched around in frilly white shirts and high-heeled boots while strumming flamenco riffs, Harry DeArmond changed the path of popular music. He marketed the first successful electric pickup, so that guitar sounds could be piped through an amplifier.

Ten years later, as if amplification weren't radical enough, DeArmond jump-started the concept of sound mods by selling the first stomp box. Actually you couldn't stomp it, the way today's guitarists use toe-operated switches to activate fuzz, sustain, flangers, and such. It looked more like an antique portable radio, with two dials on the front and a carry handle on top (above). Still, it was the world's first guitar-sound hack, fetchingly titled the DeArmond Trem Trol. As its name implied, it created tremolo.

Anyone with a strong wrist can produce tremolo manually by turning a volume control up and down 6 or 7 times a second. In other words, tremolo modulates the amplitude of the signal. This can be

Photograph by Dan Formosa

done electronically with a pair of vacuum tubes, but perhaps in an effort to cut costs, DeArmond didn't use any electronic components.

His steampunkish Trem Trol contained a motor fitted with a tapered shaft, with a rubber wheel pressing against it. The speed of the wheel varied when you turned a knob to reposition the wheel up and down the shaft. The wheel, in turn, cranked a little capsule of "hydro-fluid," in which two wires were immersed, carrying the audio signal. As the capsule rocked to and fro, the fluid sloshed from side to side, and the resistance between the electrodes fluctuated. This modulated the audio output.

Today, Trem Trols are antique collectibles. When industrial designer Dan Formosa acquired one, he found that the hydro-fluid had long since dried out, and was advised to replenish it with mercury. Somehow he didn't believe it. "I asked internet questions, and I actually went to a patent office in New York and looked up patents," he recalls. "Eventually I got word secondhand that the fluid could be replaced with Windex."

Sure enough, Windex inside works just fine, and Formosa's website at danformosa.com/dearmond.html shows how to top it off. You can even hear MP3s of the Windex-powered Trem Trol at Formosa's site and also that of Johann Burkard in Germany: makezine.com/go/burkard.

The Trem Trol started me thinking about other possibilities for a steampunk tremolo. Imagine a rotating, transparent disc. It's masked with black paint, except for a circular stripe that tapers at each end. While the disc rotates, if you shine a bright LED through the transparent stripe toward a light-dependent resistor, you'll have the basis for a tremolo device, modeled in Figure A, on the next page. You could even create never-before-heard tremolo effects by swapping discs with different stripe patterns (Figure B). For a real fabrication challenge, how about an automatic disc changer?

But, back in the real world.

Fender's Bender

In 1955, Bo Diddley became a tremolo legend using a DeArmond Model 60, and Buddy Holly followed. At this point Clarence Leonidas Fender, known as Leo, jumped on the sound-bending trend by building tremolo into his Fender amps. He named it *vibrato*, even though this term really means modulating the frequency of a note, not its amplitude.

Perhaps Fender simply wanted to protect his market share from one of his rivals, Magnatone,

which sold an amp that did have genuine vibrato. But he compounded the confusion by also introducing a "tremolo arm" for his guitars, which actually produced vibrato. Many rock musicians have been confused by the two terms ever since.

Today, transistors can create tremolo with more options and cleaner sound than the old tube amps. One of the most widely praised circuits originated in the November 1968 issue of *Electronics Australia* magazine, after which it was tickled and tweaked by a loose-knit worldwide fraternity of semi-professional circuit designers. Stomp-box authority J.D. Sleep of Raleigh, N.C., offers a modded version in kit form at his highly informative site, generalguitargadgets.com. With his permission we reprint the schematic in Figure C. (The kit version differs in some very minor details.)

Sleep has been fascinated by DIY guitar effects for most of his life. "I started to get seriously into it about 12 years ago," he says. "The web brought some 'community' to effects builders; it was a lonely hobby before then."

Describing himself as a "hands-on learner," he has no formal education in electronics and doesn't even own an oscilloscope. He recommends *Electronic Projects for Musicians* by Craig Anderton as a good starting place for people who want to experiment, and he downplays the complexity of electronics, pointing out that almost all audio schematics can be broken into blocks that have discrete functions.

In the tremolo circuit, the first block starts at the input jack and ends in the Q4 transistor stage. "This is a buffering circuit," Sleep explains, "to allow for better use with multiple effects [boxes], or a guitar with hot pickups." The second block contains Q1, which amplifies the signal, with Q2 going out to the volume control. Sleep believes the pleasing sound of the circuit is largely a function of this very clean amplifier stage.

The actual tremolo is generated by Q3, which is wired to oscillate, diverting a varying proportion of the positive audio signal to negative ground. Simple enough, but the devil is in the details, especially the component values.

"This kind of circuitry requires a lot of tweaking," Sleep notes. "Guitar audio doesn't always follow the same rules as hi-fi audio. Formulas don't always give the best guitar tone." His recommendation for beginners: "Look at schematics of effects and compare them. There is a plethora of guitar effect schematics on the web now, so this is easy and fun to do, and you can learn a lot from it."

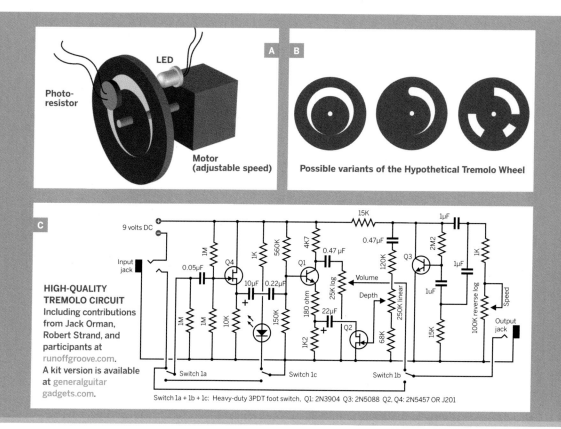

LED

Photo-resistor

Motor
(adjustable speed)

A

B

Possible variants of the Hypothetical Tremolo Wheel

C

9 volts DC

Input jack

HIGH-QUALITY TREMOLO CIRCUIT
Including contributions from Jack Orman, Robert Strand, and participants at runoffgroove.com. A kit version is available at generalguitargadgets.com.

15K

1µF

0.47µF

0.05µF

1M

Q4

1K

560K

4K7

0.47 µF

120K

2M2

Q3

1K

10µF

0.22µF

Q1

25K log

Volume

1µF

1µF

Speed

1M

1M

10K

150K

180 ohm

22µF

Depth

250K linear

68K

15K

100K reverse log

Output jack

1K2

Q2

Switch 1a

Switch 1c

Switch 1b

Switch 1a + 1b + 1c: Heavy-duty 3PDT foot switch. Q1: 2N3904 Q3: 2N5088 Q2, Q4: 2N5457 OR J201

Enter the Fuzz

A decade intervened before the next big guitar hack: distortion. Its exact origins are a matter for acrimonious debate, but everyone agrees that the Ventures made the first single using a fuzz box, titled "The 2,000 Pound Bee," in 1962. Truly awful, it used distortion merely as a gimmick and must have discouraged other musicians from taking the concept seriously.

Ray Davies of the Kinks was the first to embody distortion as an integral part of his music. He did it initially by plugging the output from one amp into the input of another, supposedly while recording his hit, "You Really Got Me." From there it was a short step to Keith Richards using a Gibson Maestro Fuzz-Tone on "(I Can't Get No) Satisfaction" in 1965.

A fuzz box creates distortion in the same way as an old-fashioned tube amplifier when someone tries to make it deliver more than its rated power. The nicely rounded sine curve from a plucked guitar string becomes "clipped" and starts to resemble a square wave (Figure D). Because a square wave contains many more harmonics (multiples of the

primary frequency), the sound becomes richer.

Transistor amps were less likely than tube amps to create this kind of distortion, so people tried to imitate the old tube sound. Today you can find thousands of advocates promoting as many different mythologies about "ideal" distortion.

I've picked a fuzz schematic from Flavio Dellepiane, a circuit designer in Italy who gives away his work (with a little help from Google AdSense) at redcircuits. com. Like J.D. Sleep, Dellepiane is self-taught, gaining much of his knowledge from electronics magazines such as the British *Wireless World*.

"I frequently searched and compared circuits to build a particular device," he recalls, "but often they were not completely fulfilling my requirements. So I was stimulated to design these circuits for myself and I started modifying them in order to obtain a result best suited to my needs."

In the case of his fuzz circuit, shown in Figure E, he used a very high-gain amplifier consisting of three field-effect transistors (FETs), which closely imitate the rounded square wave typical of an overdriven tube amp. In his words, "The distorted

Illustrations by Charles Platt

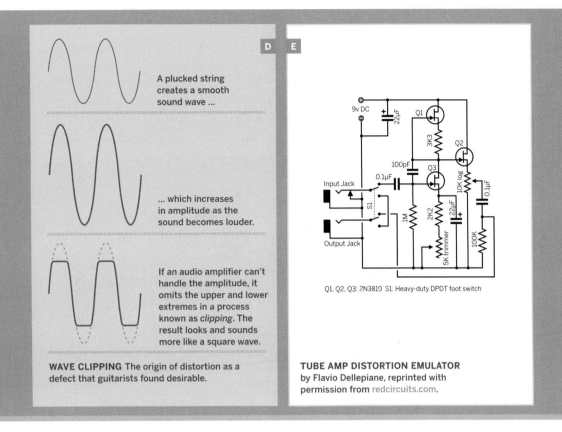

D

A plucked string creates a smooth sound wave ...

... which increases in amplitude as the sound becomes louder.

If an audio amplifier can't handle the amplitude, it omits the upper and lower extremes in a process known as *clipping*. The result looks and sounds more like a square wave.

WAVE CLIPPING The origin of distortion as a defect that guitarists found desirable.

E

9v DC
22μF
Q1
3K3
Q2
100pF
Q3
0.1μF
Input Jack
10K log
0.1μF
S1
1M
2K2
22μF
100K
Output Jack
5K trimmer

Q1, Q2, Q3: 2N3819 S1: Heavy-duty DPDT foot switch

TUBE AMP DISTORTION EMULATOR by Flavio Dellepiane, reprinted with permission from redcircuits.com.

sound obtained from such a device has a peculiar tone, much loved by most leading guitarists."

Dellepiane offers dozens more schematics on his site, developed and tested with a dual-trace oscilloscope, low-distortion sine wave oscillator (so that he can give audio devices a "clean" input), distortion meter, and precision audio voltmeter. The voltmeter and the oscillator were built from his own designs, and he gives away their schematics too. Thus his site provides one-stop shopping for home-audio electronics hobbyists in search of a self-administered education.

Guitarists today can choose from a smorgasbord of effects, all of which can be home-built using plans available online. For reference, *Analog Man's Guide to Vintage Effects* describes every vintage stomp-box and pedal you can imagine, while *How to Modify Effect Pedals for Guitar and Bass* by Brian Wampler is an extremely detailed guide for beginners.

Of course you can always take a shortcut by laying down $200 for an off-the-shelf box such as a Boss ME-20, which uses digital processing to emulate distortion, metal, fuzz, chorus, phaser,

flanger, tremolo, delay, reverb, and several more effects, all in one convenient multipedal package.

Purists, of course, will claim that homebuilt "doesn't sound the same," but maybe that's not the point. Some of us simply can't feel satisfied till we build our own stomp box and then tweak it, in search of a sound that doesn't come off-the-shelf, and is wholly our own.

Got Stomp Boxes? We've Got Mods

Since the ancient times, guitarists have modded their amps and pedals in search of that killer tone to rock your socks off. We asked DIY pedal experts what's hot in stomp box mods.

Visit makezine.com/15/stomp **for:**
» **Top 4 Easy Stomp Box Mods from Jack Orman of AMZFX**
» **Stomp box bibles**
» **Where to get parts**
» **Best web resources for DIY schematics and more**

Music at Maker Faire

Just a few of the wild and wonderful music acts at our Bay Area event. Find out more at makezine.com/go/bamfmusic2008.

Fans make music with Stephen Hobley's laser harp.

Live laptop beatjazz from Onyx Ashanti.

Pedal power from the Lee Maverick Band guitarist.

Photography by (clockwise from left): Skip Russell, Scott Beale/laughingsquid.com, and Paul Freedman

Metallic magic from Total Annihilation.

A rousing tune from the Extra Action Marching Band.

Tansy Brooks charms a snake at the Boiler Bar.

Mark Chang enchants fairgoers with his PianoMotion, simultaneously playing and steering.

Electronic Drum Kit

Velocity-sensitive impact sensors in PVC pipes interface to a micro drum machine. By Tom Zimmerman

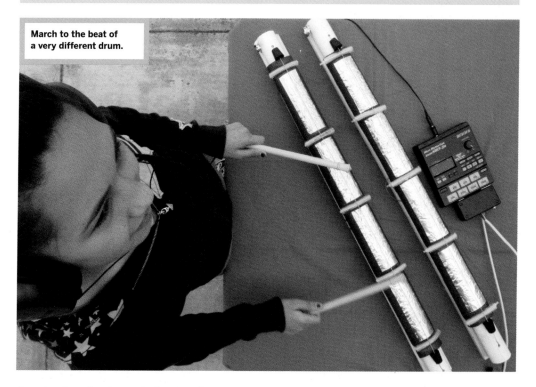

March to the beat of a very different drum.

An electronic drum is basically a switch that triggers the playback of a digitally recorded drum. Here's how I built tubular drum controllers out of PVC pipe and connected them to a studio drum machine to create a professional-sounding electronic drum kit.

Each controller has a guitar string suspended above 4 strips of aluminum tape. When you strike the string with a drumstick, it touches the tape and closes a circuit to trigger the corresponding sound from the drum machine. Foam covering the pipe softens the blow and provides a nice bounce. Underneath each controller, a pressure-sensitive piezoelectric device lifted out of the drum machine detects the force of the hit, to determine the relative volume.

The brief contact between the struck string and the foil is too short for the drum machine to detect,

so a pulse-stretching circuit lengthens the signal, by charging a capacitor.

Two male-to-female serial cables let you unplug the controllers from the drum machine. I cut the cables in half and connected them to the controllers and the drum machine. To plug-and-play, you simply mate each connector to its former other half.

Tom Zimmerman is a member of the User Sciences & Experiences Research laboratory at IBM's Almaden Research Center. An MIT graduate, he was profiled in MAKE, Volume 04.

Photograph by Sam Murphy

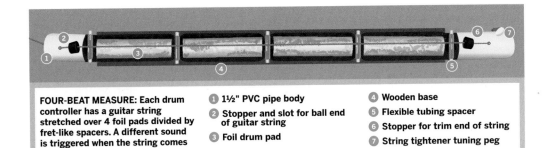

FOUR-BEAT MEASURE: Each drum controller has a guitar string stretched over 4 foil pads divided by fret-like spacers. A different sound is triggered when the string comes into contact with each pad.

1. 1½" PVC pipe body
2. Stopper and slot for ball end of guitar string
3. Foil drum pad
4. Wooden base
5. Flexible tubing spacer
6. Stopper for trim end of string
7. String tightener tuning peg

MATERIALS

Clear vinyl tubing, ½" outer diameter (OD) × ⅜" inner diameter (ID) × 5' long **Home Depot SKU #702-229; many parts available in stores are *not* listed on** homedepot.com

White polyethylene tubing, ⅜" OD × ¼" ID × 5' **Home Depot SKU #301-762**

Heat-shrink tubing

Foil tape, 1.89"×5' **Home Depot SKU #915-245**

#4 size (1" diameter) rubber bottle stoppers (4) **Home Depot SKU #755-441**

Lag screws, ¼"×1½" (6) **Home Depot SKU #654-884**

Guitar strings (2) **the thicker the better**

Guitar tuning pegs (2) **aka machine heads**

#30AWG insulated wrapping wire in 2 colors **I used RadioShack #278-501 and #278-502.**

Serial extension cables, DB9 M/F (2) **RadioShack #26-117**

11" cable ties (12) **Home Depot SKU #295-858**

Foam pipe insulation, ⅜" thick x 1⅛" ID × 6' **Home Depot SKU #420-048**

1½" PVC pipes, 36" long (2) **Home Depot SKU #193-844**

1×3 wood boards, 36" long (2)

¼"×½" bolts and matching nuts (2)

Zoom MRT-3B Micro RhythmTrak drum machine **#ZOMMRT3 from** zzounds.com, ~$100

Dual general-purpose IC PC board **RadioShack #276-159**

CD4066 quad CMOS switch, DIP package (2)

14-pin socket (2) **RadioShack #276-1999**

Project enclosure **RadioShack #270-1802**

Momentary push-button switch **RadioShack #275-1556**

Resistors: 470kΩ (8), 1kΩ (2)

0.1μF capacitors (8)

Clear silicone sealer

TOOLS

Marker

Drill and bits: 1/16", ¼", ⅜", 1"

Small flat file

Soldering iron and solder

Wire stripper

Diagonal cutters

Screwdrivers, Phillips and slotted

Pencil eraser and sandpaper

Multimeter

1. Build the controller bodies.

Our Zoom MRT-3B drum machine has 7 trigger pads and 1 bank select switch. We'll make 2 controllers to drive it, each with 4 pads. For simplicity, I'll describe building 1 controller; just double each step to make both. The controllers are physically identical, but we'll wire them slightly differently later.

1a. Draw a reference line straight down the PVC pipe; a doorjamb makes a good guide. Cut five 3" pieces each of vinyl and polyethylene tubing, then insert the polyethylene pieces into the vinyl pieces and thread a cable tie through each (Figure A, next page). These spacers will flank each drum pad.

1b. Center a 30"×3" strip of foam over the pipe's reference line and secure it down with 5 spacers, spaced 7" apart. Make sure the foam lies flat. Stick four 6" strips of foil tape to the foam, centering them between the spacers and avoiding wrinkles.

1c. Orient the pipe left-to-right, the way you'll play it. Along the reference line at the left end, drill a ¼" hole 1" from the end, and file a 1/16"-wide slot going ½" to the right (Figure B).

1d. At the right end, drill a ¼" hole along the line 1½" from the end, and another ¼" hole, for the tuning peg, on the far side of the pipe, 90° around from the line and ¾" from the end. Drill 1/16" pilot holes and install the tuning peg with the screws that came with it (Figure C). Don't overtighten or you'll strip the threads. Drill a ⅛" hole near the upper left corner of each foil pad, outside the foam and next to its adjacent cable tie.

1e. Mount the pipe to its base by turning it over and attaching the wood with 3 lag screws in countersunk holes. Solder a 6" wire to a guitar string's brass ring and slide the rubber stoppers, large ends pointing

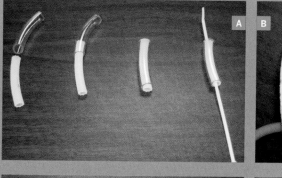
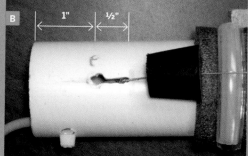

Fig. A: Nested vinyl and polyethylene tubing make fret-like spacers between drum pads. **Fig. B:** The cable end of the pipe, with a keyhole slot for the string barrel.

Fig. C: The right end of the pipe, with the tuning peg for tightening the string. **Fig. D:** Taping stripped wire to the foil drum pad.

toward each other, onto the string. Pass the wire through the slotted hole in the pipe, and anchor it by sliding the brass ring under the slot. Feed the other end of the string down through the hole at the opposite end and thread it onto the tuning peg inside. Slide 1 stopper to each end, and tighten the string so that it doesn't touch the foil.

2. Connect the pads.

2a. Feed a wire through each of the ⅛" foil pad holes and out the left end of the pipe. Strip 3" of insulation off the pad-side wires, lay the bare copper along the edge of its foil pad, and tape it down with a ¼"-wide strip of foil tape (Figure D).

NOTE: The adhesive on the bottom of the foil is non-conductive, so the copper wire must touch the top surface of the pad foil.

2b. Cut a serial cable in half. Take the female half and tie a knot 6" from the cut end. Use solder and heat-shrink tubing to connect the pad wires to the wires for serial pins 1, 2, 3, and 4, as specified in the schematic diagram, available at makezine.com/15/

electronicdrum. Pads are numbered from left to right. Use a multimeter to associate the wires in the cable with the corresponding pins on the connector.

3. Connect the piezo elements.

The Zoom MRT-3B drum machine has 2 pressure-sensitive piezoelectric elements that detect the force of pushes on its drum pad buttons. We'll remove them and put 1 underneath each pipe, so they'll perform the same function there.

3a. Pry the volume knob off the drum machine and unscrew and remove the back of the case. Remove the 4 screws inside that hold the battery case and the 2 screws on the MIDI connector. Write down where they go, and save them in a cup.

3b. The piezo elements are the disks behind the circuit board from the drum pad buttons (Figure E, bottom). Unsolder both and gently remove them. Solder and heat-shrink two 36" wires to each, and thread the wires through the side pad hole near the middle of each pipe. Slip the piezo element between

Photography by Tom Zimmerman

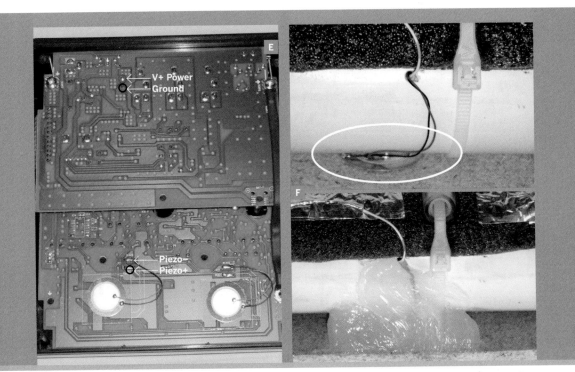

Fig. E: The piezos inside the drum machine are the 2 disks behind the drum pad button contacts.

Fig. F: The piezo element between pipe and base, before and after being encased in silicone.

the pipe and the wood, but don't force it, or it will crack. Encase the entire piezo element and its wires in silicone sealer and let it set overnight (Figure F).

3c. Following the schematic, connect the piezo's red wire to serial cable pin 7 and its black wire to pin 8. Also connect the string wire to pin 9. This completes the controller's serial cable connections. Drill two ¼" holes, one above the other, about ½" from the end of the pipe, and cable-tie the serial cable knot to the inside of the pipe (Figure G, next page).

4. Wire up the drum machine.

4a. Push the power switch into the case to dislodge the top circuit board, then unfold it to expose the board underneath. Remove the remaining screws, lift the boards from the case, and remove the white silicone pad membrane from the board along with the buttons, pads, and display. Gently sand the carbon coating off the top right corner dot of the switch pad contacts to reveal copper pads (Figure H).
CAUTION: Don't rub too hard or you'll scrape away the pads themselves.

4b. Solder 12" lengths of 30-gauge wire to the right contact of each drum pad, and pairs of wires to the Pad Bank and Function switches (Figure I). Replace the circuit boards in the case and thread the wires out the pad holes in front. Solder wire pairs to the power pads and to each of the piezo element pads on the back of the circuit boards (Figure E) and thread those out the front as well. Reassemble the drum machine in its case.

5. Build the pulse-stretching circuits.

Trim the mini PC board to fit in the project box. Clean its copper pads with a pencil eraser and solder a socket into the middle of each half. Follow the schematic to build the rest: connect the controller wires from the serial cable to the quad switch's control pins (pins 5, 6, 12, and 13), hanging a grounded 470kΩ resistor and 0.1µF capacitor off of each. Connect the quad switch's V+ (pin 14) to the controller's string (serial cable pin 9) through a 1kΩ resistor. Ground the specified quad switch pins. Finally, install both 4066 chips in the sockets.

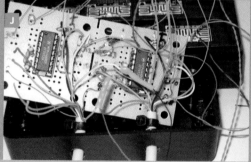

Fig. G: The drum controller's connection to the serial cable. Fig. H: Remove the coating from the upper right drum pad button contacts. Fig. I: The drum machine button pad contacts, wired. Fig. J: The pulse circuits wired to the serial cables and drum machine.

6. Connect the drum machine.

6a. Bolt the project box to the drum machine, pass the male serial cables through ¼" holes drilled in the sides, and strain-relieve them with cable ties. Mount the push-button switch on the side of the project box and solder it to the pair of wires from the drum machine's Function switch.

Follow the online schematic to connect the rest: solder the +V (pin 14) and Ground (pin 7) of one of the 4066 chips to the V+ Power and Ground of the drum machine circuit board (Figure E, previous page). Connect the pad button leads to the quad switches' signal pins. Connect the Pad Bank leads to pins 1 and 2 of controller #2 (Figure J).

6b. Plug the 2 drum controllers into the circuit, and you're ready to play. The circuit gets its power from the drum machine, so you should see its LEDs light up when you hit each pad. If they don't, swap controller cables to determine whether the problem is with the controller or the circuit. Since we wired directly to the pads, all the functions of the drum machine will still work. Pad 5 controls the Bank select. Strike it to select an alternate drum set.

Enjoy your electronic drum set. Bust out some beats and start a band!

➕ For project schematics, and video clips of disassembling a Zoom MRT-3B and playing the Electronic Drum Kit, visit makezine.com/15/electronicdrum.

Exquisite Crops

Collaborative art for the
artistically challenged.
By Charles Platt

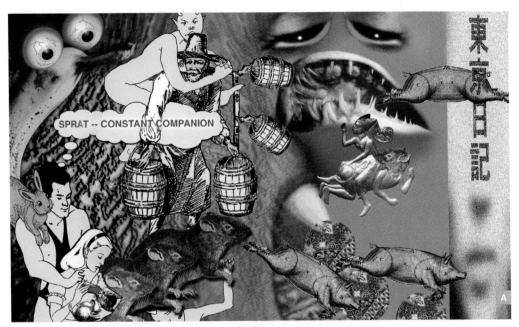

SPRAT -- CONSTANT COMPANION

Collaboration by Charles Platt, Jim Markowich, Sandra Mayer, and Richard Kadrey

Surrealist artists in the 1920s used to play a collaborative game. The first person would draw a human head at the top of a sheet of paper and then fold the paper over. The second would draw the upper half of a body, and again fold the paper over. The third and fourth artists would complete the body — at which point the paper could be unfolded, revealing the complete drawing, which they referred to as an "exquisite corpse."

As André Breton remembered the process, "Absolute nonconformism and universal disrespect was the rule, and great good humor reigned. It was a time for pleasure and nothing else." He added: "Ill-disposed critics in 1925–1930 gave further examples of their ignorance when they reproached us for delighting in such childish distractions."

Since I liked the idea of art that was fun, I pursued a similar technique with some friends during the 1990s. Then I discovered Photoshop and realized

how it could enhance the process. Each person could create a slice of the work on a separate Photoshop layer, merging the art seamlessly from one section to the next. You can do it too, even if you have little artistic ability. All you need is some clip art or a digital camera. You don't need a recent version of Photoshop, since the software has supported layers for more than a decade.

In reference to the surrealists, I named this project Exquisite Crops.

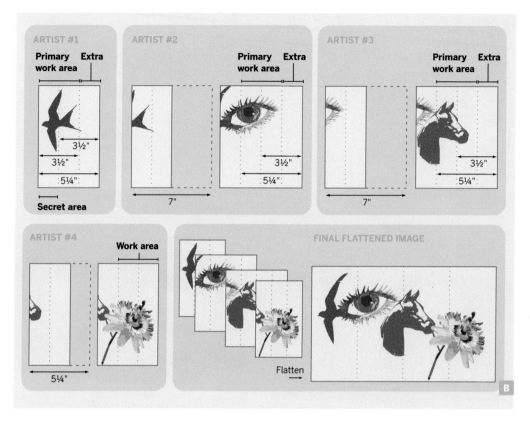

1. CHOOSE A PAPER SIZE

I like to work from left to right rather than from top to bottom, creating landscapes, which require a wide format. We found that 4 collaborators could comfortably share a legal-size sheet measuring 14"×8½". Using Photoshop, each collaborator must leave a white margin around the edge so that the result can be reproduced on a regular inkjet printer.

2. CREATE THE FIRST "SLICE"

To create the first slice, the first artist assembles images in an area 5¼" wide, subdivided into 3 equal vertical zones, each measuring 1¾" (see diagram above). The zone on the left will contain art that remains secret from the next artist. The central zone will be seen by the next artist for reference only, and should remain basically unmodified. The remaining zone on the right is an extra section that can be adapted or changed by the next artist so that everything merges together.

The first artist saves his work, then crops off the secret left-hand zone and emails the remainder to the second artist.

3. CREATE SLICES 2 AND 3

The second artist doubles the canvas size and works in the central zone, merging new art with the piece that she received from the first artist. When she finishes her work, she emails the complete file back to the first artist, who will be assembling the pieces. Then she cuts off the left half of her canvas and forwards the remainder to the third artist.

The third artist follows the same procedure as the second, as described above.

4. CREATE THE FINAL SLICE

The fourth artist extends the canvas by only 50% to complete the picture. He is the last artist, so he does not provide an extra zone for sharing. He sends his work to the first artist.

5. MERGE THE SLICES

The first artist opens each image file received from the other artists, copies and pastes each onto its own layer in a new master document, aligns them, then flattens the layers to create a single image.

Illustration by Alison Kendall

Fig. A (page 93): A completed Exquisite Crop.
Fig. B: A diagram of how to make your own digital Exquisite Crop.
Fig. C: Another project, ¾ of the way to completion; we never did find someone to finish it.
Fig. D: *Cadavre Exquis* (Exquisite Corpse) was created collaboratively by Breton and his wife, Jacqueline Lamba, with Yves Tanguy in 1938.

Even videographers and musicians have enjoyed this kind of semi-random collaborative process.

In the years since I started playing this game with software, a lot of other people have had the same idea. Check tiles.ice.org for great examples.

The game, in text form, goes all the way back to Victorian times, when it was called Consequences. Even videographers and musicians have enjoyed their own versions of it. Breton wrote that what excited him was that the works "could not be created by one brain alone, and ... were endowed with a much greater leeway, which cannot be too highly valued by poetry."

In other words, exceptional creative freedom. If you try it, I think you'll agree.

SOURCES FOR IMAGES

With a digital camera, you can capture your own source material. A scanner is good for copying found objects and images from old magazines. Google Image Search and Flickr will yield a wealth of images for almost any keyword you can think of.

Charles Platt is the Upload section editor for MAKE.

Make Your PC (Seem) Intelligent

Can your computer pass the Turing test? By Charles Platt

Can machines be intelligent? Computer pioneer Alan Turing suggested a test: put a person in front of a keyboard, communicating with a computer hidden at another location. If the computer can convince the person that he's interacting with a human being, then for all practical purposes the computer is intelligent. This came to be known as the Turing test.

The trouble is, a computer can simulate intelligence without actually being intelligent. As a very simple example, here's a tiny program that you can type in and modify, to fake the seemingly intelligent process of offering advice via proverbs.

I chose to use proverbs because I think they're not really as smart as they seem. Also, new proverbs are easy to construct because so many of them follow the same basic format of subject, verb, and outcome.

For example, if you take "pride comes before a fall" and "crime doesn't pay," you can swap their subjects to get "pride doesn't pay" or "crime comes before a fall," and the new versions still seem to make sense.

I wrote the program in BASIC (Beginner's All-purpose Symbolic Instruction Code) because even though it's an old and limited computer language, it's still the easiest for nonprogrammers to use, and it's freely available online. In the tradition of MAKE, my program encourages you to hack it. You can insert different text to create new proverbs of your own design.

1. INSTALL THE PROGRAMMING LANGUAGE

Mac users can try Chipmunk BASIC from nicholson.com/rhn/basic; the setup instructions are a little too lengthy to include here. For Windows users I suggest JustBASIC, a small but simple interpreter that costs nothing. Download it from justbasic.com/download.html and install it, and you can run it without concern for viruses.

2. DOWNLOAD THE PROVERBS CODE

Ignore the little splash screen about "The World of JustBASIC" and click the window behind it. Now you can copy-type the listing from Figure A (press Enter at the end of each line), or download our copy: *Program-pc.txt* from makezine.com/15/upload_proverbs. In the JustBASIC File menu, choose Insert File and open your downloaded copy. On the Mac, download *Program-mac.txt*, open it in a text editor, copy all the text, and paste it into the BASIC window.

3. RUN THE PROGRAM

Press Shift-F5 to run the Proverbs program (or Command-R on the Mac). If nothing seems to happen, check the status bar at the bottom of the window for messages such as "syntax error." Correct your typing and try again. When the program runs successfully, it opens its own window displaying up to 40 new proverbs without repeating any pieces of them. Because the random number generator is reseeded by the system clock near the beginning, the program is likely to create entirely different words of wisdom whenever you launch it (the total number of permutations is 1,600).

4. WRITE YOUR OWN PROVERBS

Now for the creative part. You can overwrite the current proverb text or add more. Just follow these rules:

```
dim proverb$(2,100)          data "A bird in the hand"      data "breeds contempt."
randomize time$("seconds")   data "A friend in need"        data "brings happiness."
np=40                        data "A job worth doing"       data "can work miracles."
                             data "A little knowledge"      data "cannot buy happiness."
for p=1 to 2                 data "A stolen pleasure"       data "comes before a fall."
   for q=1 to np             data "A thing of beauty"       data "comes to those who wait."
         read a$             data "Absolute power"          data "corrupts absolutely."
         proverb$(p,q)=a$    data "All work and no play"    data "costs nothing."
   next                      data "Anger"                   data "does nobody any good."
next                         data "Blind ambition"          data "doesn't pay."
                             data "Charity"                 data "has a silver lining."
q=0                          data "Crime"                   data "heals all wounds."
while q<np                   data "Curiosity"               data "hurts."
   cls:q=q+1                 data "Envy"                     data "is a dangerous thing."
   for p=1 to 2              data "Evil"                     data "is a joy forever."
      r=1+int(rnd(1)*np)     data "Generosity"              data "is a mixed blessing."
      while proverb$(p,r)="-" data "God in his wisdom"      data "is bad news."
         r=r+1:if r>np then r=1 data "Haste"                data "is best forgotten."
      wend                   data "Heaven above"            data "is better than nothing."
      print proverb$(p,r);" "; data "Hindsight"            data "is bliss."
      proverb$(p,r)="-"      data "Honesty"                 data "is cheap."
   next                      data "Impulsive behavior"      data "is good news."
   print:print              data "Jealousy"                 data "is its own reward."
   print"Press Enter for another," data "Love"             data "is next to godliness."
   print"or X to exit: ";   data "Misery"                  data "is only skin deep."
   k=0                       data "Money"                   data "is often spoken in jest."
   do                        data "Much ado about nothing"  data "is sweet."
      k=asc(input$(1))       data "One good turn"           data "is the best medicine."
   loop until k=88 or k=120 or k=13  data "Pride"          data "is the best policy."
   if k<>13 then q=np        data "Procrastination"         data "is the root of all evil."
wend                         data "Regret"                  data "is the path to wisdom."
cls:end                      data "Revenge"                 data "is a thing of beauty."
                             data "Selfishness"             data "justifies the means."
                             data "Success"                 data "kills."
                             data "The devil you know"      data "lasts forever."
                             data "The darkest hour"        data "leads to a life of regret."
```

A

Fig. A: In JustBASIC the program listing should look like this (it will appear in one long column). **Fig. B:** Sample output from the Proverbs program.

```
Sample output from the Proverbs program:

Absolute power is a dangerous thing.
The darkest hour makes you stronger.
Curiosity is the root of all evil.
Impulsive behavior is best forgotten.
Anger cannot buy happiness.
Envy leads to a life of regret.
Haste comes before a fall.
Love pleases no one.
Heaven above is better than nothing.
God in his wisdom kills.
Crime is a thing of beauty.
```

B

» Every piece of a proverb must be inside quotation marks on a line that begins with the word data followed by a space.
» The first and second blocks of data must contain an equal number of lines.
» If you change that number, you must substitute your new value instead of the number 40 in the statement np=40 on line 3 of the program.

I've reproduced some samples of the output in Figure B. I especially like Anger cannot buy happiness and The darkest hour makes you stronger. I'm intrigued by God in his wisdom kills, but a bit skeptical about Crime is a thing of beauty. What pseudointelligent combinations can your version of the program create?

Back in the day — which was during the 1980s — computer magazines published a lot of listings like this, and some people who got hooked on BASIC went on to become career programmers. Not so many people play with BASIC anymore, but it's still fun and is well suited to natural-language processing. If you want to understand how it works, study one of the many online tutorials. Then you can try to build your own artificial-intelligence software to accept user input and cycle it back in seemingly meaningful responses.

Maybe you can even write software that passes the Turing test — although so far, no one has succeeded.

BASIC Incompatibilities

Computer languages have regional dialects, like human languages. The idiosyncrasies of JustBASIC include the peculiar syntax on line 2 of the listing, which reseeds the random number generator. It also allows the commands do and loop, which are not universal. If you try to run this program using a different interpreter, you may need to rewrite these lines. If you modify the program in JustBASIC you should be aware that it doesn't allow you to read data directly into an array, and its input$() function doesn't recognize the Esc key.

For a really powerful version of BASIC that accesses all the features of Windows, I recommend PowerBASIC, which is extremely fast and versatile.

Charles Platt is a section editor for MAKE.

Make Yourself Invisible

Anyone can now acquire a bulletproof, anonymous online identity. By Publius

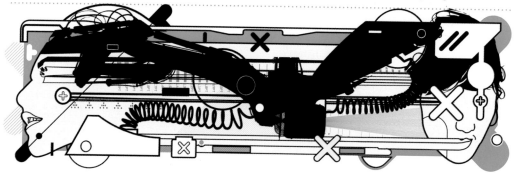

In May of this year, a judge ordered Facebook to turn over the identity of someone who created a fake profile of a high school official. Other school officials have sued over fake MySpace profiles. Not all judges take free speech rights seriously; even fewer high school and university administrators do. Setting up an anonymous blog or website is the obvious way to protect yourself from being punished for speaking out, but is this legitimate? And if so, how can you accomplish it?

Anonymous speech has a long and distinguished history. It was part of the political debate leading to the rift with Great Britain; revolutionaries relied on it to conceal their identities from the Crown.

The tradition continued with the Federalist Papers, which presented arguments for ratifying the U.S. Constitution. They were published in the 1780s under pseudonyms including "Publius." The authors of the Anti-Federalist Papers, who predicted that the Constitution would lead to a tyrannical central government, used aliases including "Federal Farmer."

Internet anonymity is something of a high-wire tightrope act: one tiny technological misstep, and you're doomed. Fortunately, technologies for anonymous website publishing are both secure and, finally, easy to use.

You can create an anonymous or pseudonymous persona that's proof against not just random busybodies, but attorneys armed with subpoenas too. (You should be familiar with relevant state and federal laws, of course, and do nothing illegal.)

Today, online anonymity works by cloaking your computer's Internet Protocol (IP) address, which can be traced back to you in some circumstances. One way to cloak your IP address is to use someone else's, such as a local coffee shop, corporation, or neighborhood home with an open wi-fi connection. But that's not terribly convenient, and a business may not be delighted to find out what you're doing (even if an open access point was their mistake).

A better solution is free software named Tor that lets you connect to a sophisticated network of anonymizing servers, meaning your IP address will appear to be the address of a Tor server, not your own. Messages are encrypted and forwarded randomly through the Tor network before they reach their destination.

At the cost of some speed, this arrangement provides pretty good privacy protection — there are no absolute guarantees — against attempts to unearth the identity of who's behind an email address or website.

Illustration by Julian Honoré/p4rse.com

1. DOWNLOAD TOR SOFTWARE

Go to torproject.org and download the latest stable version of Tor for your system (Figure A); as of this writing it was 0.1.2.19. It's available for Windows, Mac OS X, and a number of Linux/Unix systems. Follow the installation instructions, which may require a reboot.

At this point you should create a user account for our anonymous identity (Figure B). This may seem like overkill, but it helps to ensure that your browser isn't leaking information about your identity by, for instance, sending your existing cookies to a web-based email service or publishing tool. Another option is to create a second browser profile. If you're using Firefox, check out support.mozilla.com/en-us/kb/profiles.

2. INSTALL FIREFOX'S TORBUTTON ADD-ON

You're not done setting up Tor yet. If you're using Firefox, which I highly recommend, go to add-ons, addons.mozilla.org/en-us/firefox, and install the Torbutton add-on (Figure C, next page). The main Tor website has instructions on how to configure other browsers such as Safari.

Start up the graphical front-end to Tor, which is called Vidalia, and restart Firefox. You should see a box on the bottom right of each Firefox window saying "Tor Disabled" in red. Click on it and it should say "Tor Enabled" in green.

3. VERIFY THAT TOR IS WORKING

Before you trust Tor with your privacy, verify that it's actually working. Turn it off, visit ipid.shat.net, and note what IP address it lists as yours. Then activate Tor and reload that page. Your IP address that's visible to the outside world should have changed.

4. CREATE A HUSHMAIL ACCOUNT

I recommend using Hushmail (hushmail.com) for a web-based email account (Figure D, next page). All connections are encrypted, and it functions well with Tor. No existing email address is required. (If you really want to use Gmail, then create an account and log into it by visiting https://mail.google.com/mail. The "https" part of this URL insures that your connections will be encrypted.)

Tor: anonymity online

Tor is a software project that helps you defend against traffic analysis, a form of network surveillance that threatens personal freedom and privacy, confidential business activities and relationships, and state security. Tor protects you by bouncing your communications around a distributed network of relays run by volunteers all around the world: it prevents somebody watching your Internet connection from learning what sites you visit, and it prevents the sites you visit from learning your physical location. Tor works with many of your existing applications, including web browsers, instant messaging clients, remote login, and other applications based on the TCP protocol.

Hundreds of thousands of people around the world use Tor for a wide variety of reasons: journalists and bloggers, human rights workers, law enforcement officers, soldiers, corporations, citizens of repressive regimes, and just ordinary citizens. See the Who Uses Tor? page for examples of typical Tor users. See the overview page for a more detailed explanation of what Tor does, why this diversity of users is important, and how Tor works.

There are three pieces of fine print you need to know about.

1. Tor does not protect you if you do not use it correctly. Read our list of warnings and make sure to follow the instructions for your platform carefully.
2. Even if you configure and use Tor correctly, there are still potential attacks that could compromise Tor's ability to protect you.
3. No anonymity system is perfect these days, and Tor is no exception: you should not rely solely on the current Tor network if you really need strong anonymity.

Tor's security improves as its user base grows and as more people volunteer to run relays. (It isn't nearly as hard to set up as you might think, and can significantly enhance your own security against some attacks.) If running a relay isn't for you, we need help with many other aspects of the project, and we need funds to continue making the Tor network faster and easier to use while maintaining good security. Please donate.

A

B

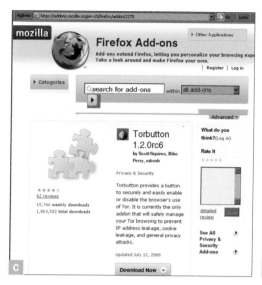

Encryption is important. Because of the way the Tor network works, the last Tor server your communications flow through can see whatever you're doing. Some snarky server operators even have posted lightly edited logs of usernames and passwords they've gleaned. An encrypted connection protects you from this kind of eavesdropping.

The primary downside with Hushmail is that you have to log into your account at least once every 3 weeks or it will be deactivated. Upgrading it to a paid version solves that problem, but the federal government has made it tricky to transfer funds anonymously. (Hushmail does accept the Liberty Reserve online payment system and, of course, money orders sent through the post.)

5. CREATE A BLOGGER ACCOUNT

Creating a new blog is straightforward enough, but anonymous publishing involves some twists. First, I've had some problems recently using Tor and WordPress — cookies don't seem to be passed through properly — and wouldn't recommend it. Fortunately, Google's Blogger (blogger.com) works nicely with Tor and doesn't even require an email address to get started.

Second, to make it more difficult to identify the author, you should time your posts to appear a few minutes or hours in the future. Otherwise you risk the unpleasant situation of a network administrator

> Internet anonymity is a high-wire tightrope act: one tiny technological misstep, and you're doomed.

(perhaps at a school or corporation) learning that you've been connecting to Tor at the precise time a blog entry was posted.

If you feel like giving something back to the unpaid volunteers who made your anonymous web browsing possible, you can become one yourself by configuring Vidalia to relay traffic. And the Tor Project happily accepts donations at torproject.org/donate.

Publius prefers to write anonymously about anonymity.

Stain Palette

I mix tiny amounts of touch-up stains in those little plastic artist palettes. They have six wells that hold about a teaspoon each. I don't clean up after using it, but instead "reactivate" the stain with solvent next time I need a little dab. It's a great way to have a variety of colors available at the ready.   —Frank Joy

Find more tools-n-tips at makezine.com/tnt.

Make: Projects

Need some air? Pierce the sky with a bike-pump-powered air rocket you can shoot within city limits. Or make rings around people with three different versions of the vortex cannon, launching toroids out of thin air. Power hungry? Juice up small electronic devices with waste heat from a candle, using a steampunk Seebeck generator built from scrap.

Photograph by Gabriela Hasbun

COMPRESSED AIR ROCKET
By Rick Schertle

PAPER, TAPE, COMPRESSED AIR ... LIFT-OFF!

Blow your friends away as you send this 25-cent rocket hundreds of feet in the air. You can build this easy launcher and rocket with common hardware store items in an afternoon.

All the parts for this simple but impressive air rocket and launcher are cheap and easy to find. Building it is a breeze and the modifications are endless. It's legal in a big city, reusable, clean, and can be launched even in high winds on a small field.

Believe me, folks are quite taken by the 200- to 300-foot flights fueled by 18 or so bicycle pumps of compressed air. Whether you're launching on your own or with a whole group of rocketeers, watch the crowds gather ... 3, 2, 1, and away!

! CAUTION: DANGEROUS PROJECT
At normal temperatures, standard Schedule 40 PVC has a working pressure of around 150psi, but heat, sunlight, solvents, scratches, and time make the material lose strength, and even at the 75psi used for this project, it will eventually fail. When it fails, it will break into fragments that can be thrown with great force by the compressed air. For added safety, wear safety goggles and wrap PVC elements in several layers of duct tape (not shown) to minimize any possible shrapnel. For a bomb-proof model, you could also build the entire system out of galvanized steel pipe at a greater expense.

Set up: p.105   Make it: p.106   Use it: p.113

Photograph by Gabriela Hasbun

Rick Schertle (schertle@yahoo.com) is a master at the craft of teaching middle school in San Jose and a novice maker at home. His diverse interests include backyard chickens, adventure travel, veggie oil-fueled cars, and geocaching — all made more fun with the enthusiastic support of his wife and the crazy antics of his young son and daughter.

PUMP IT UP, UP, AND AWAY!

AIR ROCKET ANATOMY

1 **Bicycle pump**

2 **Tire valve** Allows PVC chamber to be pressurized.

3 **¾" inline electric sprinkler valve** Releases the pressure in an instant burst.

4 **Paired wires** Connect the battery button and sprinkler valve.

5 **Button** Triggers the sprinkler valve for the launch.

6 **R/C toy or power tool battery** Provides the juice necessary to trigger the valve under pressure.

My 5-year-old son demonstrated the physics of an air rocket recently at a hamburger joint when he shot the wrapper off his soda straw. That's basically how this air rocket works.

The launcher is made from PVC pipe, and has a chamber that's pressurized using a bicycle pump. The pressure is released in a split second through an electric sprinkler valve, sending the paper-and-tape rocket into the sky.

What's unique about this design (as opposed to a solid-fuel model rocket or soda-bottle water rocket) is that the force of the air propelling the rocket upward is applied all at once. It still blows my mind that just this initial blast of air can send the rocket so high.

If you want more info on the basic physics of the air rocket, this NASA link gives a nice simple description: makezine. com/go/airnasa. NASA's description of how air-powered rockets work also includes a nice Flash animation.

~18x

4.8V
600mAh

Illustration by Nik Schulz

SET UP.

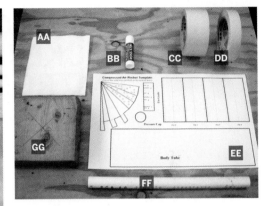

MATERIALS

[A] ¾" PVC slip end caps (2) **see below**

[B] ¾" PVC adapters, ¾" male threaded × ¾" female slip (2)

[C] ¾" PVC reducers: ¾" male slip × ½" female threaded and ½" female slip × ¾" male slip

[D] 2" PVC slip tee

[E] 2" PVC slip end cap

[F] 2" PVC reducer bushings, male slip × ¾" female slip (2)

[G] 2" PVC pipe, 10" length

[H] ¾" PVC pipe, 3" and 4" lengths

[I] ½" PVC pipe, 16" length **for launch tube**

[J] 48" length of 1×3 pine board **to be cut to various sizes for the launch tower**

[K] 10' length of paired wire **I used speaker wire.**

[L] Button momentary switch **RadioShack part #275-609**

[M] Tire air valve

[N] Teflon tape

[O] Electrical tape

[P] Wood screws, size #6×1½" or similar (8)

[Q] 10' length of 5/16" (outside diameter) × 3/16" (inside diameter) flexible vinyl tubing

[R] ¼" hex bolts, 2" long (2), wing nuts (2), and washers (4)

[S] PVC cement and primer

[T] 24"×24" piece of ½" plywood **as a base for the launch tower**

[U] ¾" inline 24V electric sprinkler valve **Cheap is fine, just make sure you get an inline one.**

[V] Hose clamps: size #4, 7/16"–11/16" (2) and size #72, 3½"–5" (2)

[W] ½" male threaded × 1/8" female threaded brass reducer bushing

[X] 3/16" hose barb × 1/8" male threaded brass fitting

[NOT SHOWN]
Battery connector
Connectors can be the standard R/C toy type used for rechargeable batteries, or a generic bullet type.

Power tool or R/C toy battery to trigger the sprinkler valve. Under pressure, the valve requires higher amperage: a power tool or R/C toy battery will work, minimum 4.8V, 600mAh.

Bicycle pump and pressure gauge Use a pump with a built-in gauge, or just use an ordinary pen-type tire pressure gauge.

ROCKET BUILDING MATERIALS
[AA] Paper napkin

[BB] Glue stick

[CC] 2"-wide masking tape

[DD] ¾"-wide masking tape

[EE] Printed rocket template **Download it from** makezine.com/15/airrocket **and print on 8½"×14" paper.**

[FF] 13" length of ½" PVC pipe **for rocket-building stand**

[GG] 5½" length of scrap 2×6 lumber

TOOLS

[NOT SHOWN]
Hacksaw or PVC cutter
A cheap PVC cutter is a super handy tool for cutting hose, PVC pipe, etc.

Fine sandpaper

Rubber mallet

Utility knife

Screwdrivers

Drill and bits: 3/32", ¼", ½", 13/16"

Saw for cutting lumber to various sizes

Soldering iron and solder (optional)

Socket set (optional)

Scissors

Wire cutters

Adjustable wrench

Channel-lock pliers

Large C-clamp

Please note: Only Schedule 40 PVC should be used.

Photography by Rick Schertle

MAKE IT.

BUILD YOUR AIR ROCKET LAUNCHER AND ROCKETS

START »

Time: **An Afternoon** Complexity: **Easy**

1. ASSEMBLE THE PRESSURE CHAMBER

1a. Use PVC primer, then cement, to glue the 2" male slip × ¾" female slip PVC reducer bushing into the 2" slip tee. Next, prime and glue the ¾" male slip × ½" female threaded PVC reducer into the 2" male slip × ¾" female slip PVC reducer bushing.

1b. Apply teflon tape to the threads of both brass fittings. Screw the brass barbed fitting to the brass ½"×⅛" reducer bushing. Screw the ½"×⅛" brass reducer bushing into the ¾" male slip × ½" female threaded PVC reducer. Tighten all connections with an adjustable wrench.

1c. To complete the pressure chamber assembly, prime and glue the 2" end cap onto the 10" length of 2" PVC pipe. Next, glue the 10" piece of 2" pipe into the other end of the 2" tee as shown.

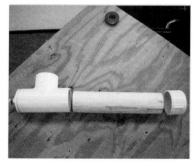

2. BUILD THE LAUNCH SYSTEM

2a. Wrap teflon tape around each of the ¾" male threaded × ¾" female slip PVC adapters. Thread the adapters onto the ¾" inline 24V electric sprinkler valve and tighten with channel-lock pliers.

2b. Cut a 3" length of ¾" PVC and a 16" length of ½" PVC. Glue the 3" piece into the "In" side of the sprinkler valve. Glue the ¾" male slip × ½" female slip reducer and the 16" length of ½" PVC into the "Out" side of the valve.

2c. Glue the 2" male slip × ¾" female slip PVC reducer bushing into the tee on the pressure chamber.

2d. Glue the completed launch assembly into the pressure chamber. Your air launch system is complete.

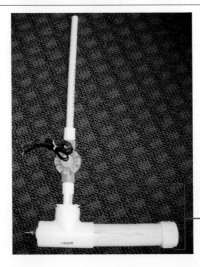

⚠ **WARNING: Wrap the pressure chamber with several layers of duct tape (not shown) to prevent injury in case the chamber shatters under pressure.**

3. BUILD THE LAUNCH TOWER AND ATTACH THE LAUNCH SYSTEM

3a. Cut your ¾"×3" lumber to the following lengths: 15" (1), 3½" (2), and 12" (2).

3b. Clamp a 3½" length to the 15" length as shown. Pre-drill 2 holes with the ³/₃₂" bit and then screw in the 1½" screws using a drill/driver. A bit of wood glue would be good too, if available. Repeat with the other 3½" length on the other side.

3c. Mark a 3½" piece 1" from the bottom, mark a 12" piece 2" from the top, line them up, and sandwich them together using a C-clamp. Drill a ¼" hole through both pieces, then slip a ¼" hex bolt through, with washers on both sides and a wing nut on the outside. Repeat on the other side.

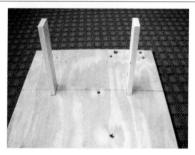

3d. The 24"×24" piece of plywood will provide a sturdy base for the launch tower. Measure and mark a line down the center of the plywood, 12" in from either side. On your centerline, measure and mark 4½" in from both ends. Place the legs of the launch tower with their edges on the inside of the marks, then trace a line around each leg. Drill two ³/₃₂" holes in each traced area.

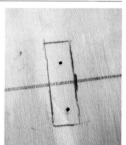

3e. Turn the whole thing upside down, line up the launch tower on the marks, and then finish drilling pilot holes into the launch tower legs, through the existing holes in the plywood. Screw into place.

3f. Once your base is secure, attach the pressure chamber/launch system to the horizontal board using the 2 large hose clamps. Your launch tower is complete.

4. MAKE AND WIRE THE LAUNCH BUTTON

4a. Drill a ¼" hole in the middle of one ¾" PVC slip end cap, and drill a ½" hole in the middle of the other to accommodate the button switch.

4b. Thread the paired wire through the end cap with the smaller hole, from the outside, and tie a knot about 8" from the end, so the knot is inside the cap. Now thread the end of the wire in the following order — through the 4" piece of ¾" PVC, through the nut and washer for the button, then through the ½" hole in the other ¾" end cap, from the inside.

4c. Solder the wire ends to the leads on the bottom of the button. Slip the washer and nut over the button, inside the PVC cap, and tighten the nut using a pair of needlenose pliers. This can be a bit tricky.

4d. Push everything together to complete the button assembly. Don't glue it, in case you need to make repairs to your button later.

4e. Connect the wiring. Solder connections when possible, and insulate them with electrical tape.

1. Use bullet connectors or something similar to connect the battery leads to the button and the electric valve.
2. Connect 1 wire from the button to 1 lead on the sprinkler valve. Twist, then solder and/or tape.
3. Connect the other wire from the button to one of the bullet connectors on the battery leads (red or black, it doesn't matter).
4. Connect the remaining battery connector to the remaining lead on the sprinkler valve.

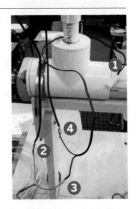

4f. Tape the wire for the button to the vertical support of the launch tower. Test your launch button. When you press the button, you should hear the sprinkler valve click open and closed. You'll do more testing later when the system is under pressure.

5. MAKE THE AIR HOSE AND TEST THE LAUNCH SYSTEM

5a. Now we're going to assemble and attach the air hose to the launcher. First, strip the rubber off the tire valve. You can use fine sandpaper to clean off the valve so it's shiny.

5b. Slip the tiny hose clamp over the hose and insert the tire valve into the hose. Push it in as far as you can. Tighten the hose clamp over the tube and valve using a socket or screwdriver. This connection was the Achilles' heel in my prototype launcher. Granted, it was exciting to have the hose explode off at 75psi, hissing wildly like a snake, but, for the sake of reliability, I've strengthened it by using the mini hose clamps.

Slip the second mini hose clamp over the other end of the hose, and push the hose end onto the ³⁄₁₆" hose barb. Tighten the clamp over the hose and barb. If you find the clamp too big and you're not able to get it really tight, wrap the barb in rubber from a bike inner tube and then tighten the clamp over that.

5c. Attach the bicycle pump to the tire valve and pressurize the system to about 75psi. Keep an eye on the gauge and listen for any hissing. The pressure should stay at 75psi. If you find leaks, fix them and try again.

Release the pressure by pressing the launch button (with the battery connected). **Be careful when you do this — wear eye protection and stand clear of the pressure chamber.**

If the pressure doesn't release when you press the button, tighten down the solenoid (the black thing with the wires coming out) on the sprinkler valve. You may also need a larger battery (one with more amps) to trigger the solenoid under pressure.

If you're still having problems with your electrical system, most valves have a manual trigger you can flip to release the pressure. If you're up this close to the valve you may want hearing protection as well. **Be very careful that your head is away from the launch tube.**

6. BUILD THE ROCKET ASSEMBLY STAND

Mark the center of a 5½" scrap of 2×6 lumber. Drill a ¹³⁄₁₆" hole 1" deep in the center. This is where a drill press is really handy. Then twist a 13" length of ½" PVC pipe into the hole. Add masking tape to the base of the pipe, if needed, to get a snug fit.

7. BUILD THE ROCKETS

7a. Download the rocket template from makezine.com/15/airrocket and print it out on 8½"×14" paper. Cut out all the pieces on the solid lines as shown.

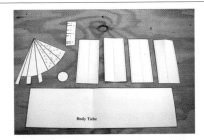

7b. Wrap the body tube around the assembly stand and tape it in 5 places with the ¾" masking tape. The smoother your tape, the more aerodynamic your rocket will be. Now wrap the body tube with 2" masking tape, working your way down. Slide the body tube to the top of the PVC stand. Tape the pressure cap on top of the body tube by crisscrossing ¾" tape over the top, and smooth it down.

NOTE: Make sure to overlap the tape, making it about 2 layers thick everywhere. If you miss a spot, you'll have a dramatic blowout!

7c. Curl the nose cone around to overlap the dotted section, and tape it in place. Stuff the nose cone tightly with the napkin. A full napkin should fit in. Use a pencil to pack it tightly.

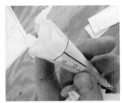

7d. Place the nose cone on top of the body tube, tape around the tabs, then cover the nose cone in tape.

7e. Wrap the fin guide around the PVC pipe at the base of the body tube and mark on the 3s for a 3-fin model or the 4s for 4 fins.

7f. Fold the fins on the dashed lines, then stack them together and trim the tops and bottoms at an angle.

7g. Glue the fins together with a glue stick, and pinch them to adhere them. Make sure you don't glue the tabs that will be used to attach the fins to the rocket.

7h. Line up the fins with the marks on the bottom of the body tube. Tape all fins securely in place.

Your rocket is now complete and ready to launch. The great thing about these rockets is that no matter how they're built, they will fly! Some of course will fly better than others, but they all will fly to some degree.

FINISH X

ROCKET SAFETY, SITE SELECTION, OPERATION, AND CONTESTS

SAFETY

As with any air-powered device, you have to use caution. Eye injuries are your biggest danger. Safety goggles for you and any spectators are required.

SITE SELECTION

Because these air rockets have no recovery system, you can launch them in a fairly small area even with wind. They will go very high but then come right back down.

A small field would be an ideal launch site. The rockets are light and soft, so while it's not ideal for them to land on cars, the chance of damage is slight.

OPERATION

Set the launcher on the ground and lay out the air hose and launch button wire away from the launcher.

Slide the rocket down the launch tube until it stops at the pressure cap. This is a tight fit and you may need to smooth down the inside bottom of the rocket with your fingers to get it on. You may also bevel the top of the PVC launch tube with a file to make it easier.

Connect the air pump to the hose and pump up to about 75psi. If you go above 75psi, you may blow out the side of your rocket.

Count down and then launch! With a good launch, the rocket will go nearly out of sight and then free-fall to the ground.

The rocket will get crumpled as it hits the ground, but can simply be pinched back into shape and launched again and again.

If for some reason it does not launch, follow the pressure testing instructions in Step 5c.

> **⚠ CAUTION:** When placing the rocket on the launcher, make sure your head is never over the launch tube. Wear safety goggles. Make sure everyone is clear from the area before launching, and do a countdown once everyone is at a safe distance.

CONTESTS

» Tilt the launch tower, then place a trash can 100yds away and see who can get the closest.

» Build a simple clinometer (wikihow.com/Make-a-Clinometer) and have contests to see whose rocket can get the highest.

OTHER RESOURCES

If this MAKE project really grabs you, here's a great article on air rockets and some more sophisticated setups, by two professors at Southern Illinois University: makezine.com/go/airrocket.

VORTEX CANNONS

By Edwin Wise

DOING DONUTS

A smoke ring, or vortex, is a beguiling thing to watch: a coherent, moving structure made out of thin air. Here are 3 cannons that can throw these "chunks of air" across a room.

I'd been aware of vortex cannons for quite some time, mostly as an interesting toy, and after I kept stumbling on the concept while touring the web, I decided I had to build my own. There's something fascinating about taking a substance as ubiquitous and amorphous as air and transforming it into a coherent and persistent structure, almost like a crystal. I also hoped to find some use for my cannon, perhaps to propel scents or give the touch of a ghost in a haunted house.

An extreme example of the vortex's "reach out and touch someone" power is the military vortex gun, which uses explosives to drive air rings that can knock people over, or at least generate enough sound pressure to render an area uninhabitable. And the Shockwave Cannon created by Survival Research Labs delivers an invisible boot to the head.

This project doesn't go that far, but it will show you how to make 3 different cannons: a 5-minute version, a computer-controlled version driven by a subwoofer, and a powerful one based on my Boom Stick project (*MAKE, Volume 13, page 114*).

Set up: p.117   Make it: p.118   Use it: p.121

Edwin Wise is a software engineer with more than 25 years of professional experience developing software by day and exploring the edges of mad science by night. He can be found at simreal.com.

TOROID AFFAIRS

TOROID

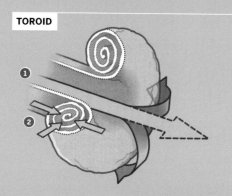

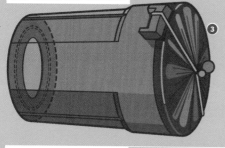

HOW IT WORKS

Just as a sphere (ball) is the natural shape for solids to roll on a surface, the toroid (donut) is the natural shape for a gas to "roll" axially through space.

As air moves forward through the toroid's inside edge, it draws air back around from the outside edge to replace it. The moving air exerts less pressure than the still air around it, so it stays in the donut shape.

Making a traveling vortex is easy: just push a puff of air evenly through a wide circular aperture. As the puff emerges, surrounding air travels in to fill the low-pressure zone behind it. This pinches it off and curls it back on itself to form the ring. You can make the ring visible by using smoke or fog from a fog machine.

An empty, topless gallon milk jug will make a vortex if you thump its bottom. The "Tub Thumping" cannon here is a larger version based on a garbage can.

The "Barking Tube" cannon uses a subwoofer to push out a series of vortices. The velocity curve of the impulse affects the vortex ring: an accelerating push makes it fly faster, while a decelerating push adds spin, making it fly slower and disintegrate dramatically.

The "Big Bad Boom" cannon (instructions online at makezine.com/15/vortex) launches a vortex strong enough to travel outdoors (if it isn't windy).

TUB THUMPING CANNON

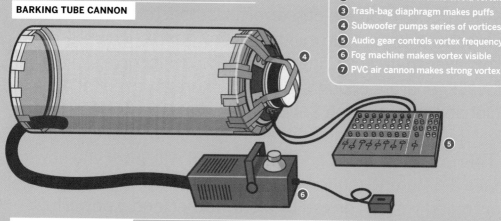

1. Puff of air travels forward
2. Low pressure aft forms toroid vortex
3. Trash-bag diaphragm makes puffs
4. Subwoofer pumps series of vortices
5. Audio gear controls vortex frequency
6. Fog machine makes vortex visible
7. PVC air cannon makes strong vortex

BARKING TUBE CANNON

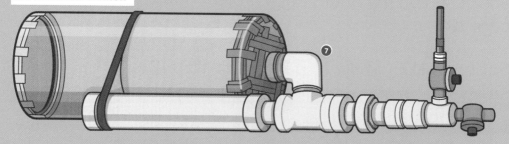

BIG BAD BOOM CANNON

Illustration by Damien Scogin

SET UP.

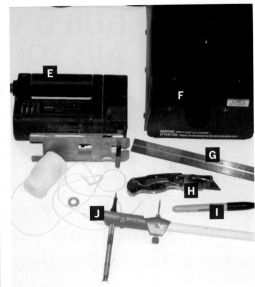

MATERIALS

TUB THUMPING CANNON

[A] 32-gallon plastic trash can with lid

[B] 45-gallon trash bag or tarp

[C] Ball, 1"–2" diameter

[D] Bungee cords (2), 1 small, 1 large

BARKING TUBE CANNON
[MATERIALS NOT SHOWN]

½" plywood, 24"×24" sheet

¾" polystyrene insulating foam

Duct tape

Strong adhesive such as Liquid Nails or epoxy

12"-diameter cardboard tube, about 2' long

12"-diameter subwoofer speaker

Audio wave signal source I used a laptop running Tone Generator from NCH Software (nch.com.au/tonegen).

Audio power amplifier

BIG BAD BOOM CANNON

This cannon is based on the Boom Stick project from MAKE, Volume 13. See makezine.com/15/vortex for the materials list and instructions.

TOOLS

[E] Jigsaw

[F] Party/Halloween fog machine

[G] Ruler

[H] Sharp knife

[I] Felt-tip marker

[J] 12" compass, or string, a washer, and a wood screw

Photography by Edwin Wise

MAKE IT.

BUILD YOUR AIR TOROID CANNONS

START ⋙

Time: Various Complexity: Easy

1. TUB THUMPING VORTEX CANNON

This simple cannon, which you can make in 5 minutes, is a good way to get started.

1a. Cut a 6" hole in the bottom of the trash can. That's it — you're done! Now you can fill the can with fog from the party fogger and generate vortexes by thumping on the lid.

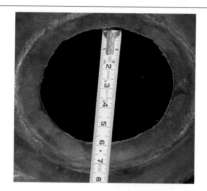

Photography by Edwin Wise

1b. The trash can's lid will only take this abuse for so long before it cracks and falls apart. You can replace it with a snappy new plastic diaphragm. Start by gathering the center of a trash bag or tarp around a ball and using a small bungee cord to tie it off into a knob.

TIP: A light thump makes a slow-moving vortex, while a hard thump makes a fast-moving but less stable vortex.

1c. Duct-tape the diaphragm all around the top of the can with the knob in the center, leaving some slack. Stretch the large bungee cord across the handles. To fire, pull back and release the knob.

NOTE: You can experiment by cutting the hole larger. This makes larger vortexes that move more slowly.

2. BARKING TUBE VORTEX CANNON

This computer-controlled cannon was inspired by Bill Beaty's Amateur Science website (amasci.com/amasci.html).

2a. Tape a 12" subwoofer into 1 end of a 12" cardboard tube.

2b. Wire the speaker to an amplifier, and wire the amp to your audio source. I used a laptop running Tone Generator, downloadable at nch.com.au/tonegen.

2c. Cut a plywood or foam ring for the exhaust end of the barrel, with an inside diameter between 4" and 6". Glue and tape it into place. This ring creates the vortex, and controls its size and velocity.

2d. Fill the barrel with fog and play saw-tooth waves in the 1Hz to 10Hz range. Admire your vortices. Experiment with the frequency; when it gets too fast, the rings blur together and lose their structure.

3. BIG BAD BOOM VORTEX CANNON

My Boom Stick PVC air cannon, from MAKE, Volume 13, is great for generating air vortices. You just need to add a bit more plumbing and a large cardboard tube. See makezine.com/15/vortex for details.

USE IT.

FLYING FACTS FOR ROLLING DONUTS

EXPLORING THE VORTEX

With the computer-controlled Barking Tube, I wanted to experiment with different waveforms that would slowly pull the speaker cone back, and then fire it forward in a shaped pulse. I wrote a waveform generator in Java, but unfortunately found that the speaker wouldn't follow the form. Instead, the cone moves in one "bounce" which pulls the smoke ring back into the cannon before it can detach and fly away. Either the audio synth in my computer or the amplifier itself filtered out most of the signal's very-low-frequency components, distorting my waveform beyond any use. So I ended up using regular sawtooth waves, which work, but the only parameter to play with is the frequency. More work is needed.

The Big Bad Boom version will work outside, but the others work only in still air; a breeze will break up the vortex structure. In general, faster and smaller vortices dissipate sooner than slower and larger ones. In a controlled, still environment, a big, slow vortex can travel a long distance. In my not-so-controlled garage, I got Big Bad Boom vortices to travel 10'–20'.

The cannons are primarily meant for fun, and to illustrate the physics of the vortex. Any potential practical uses come from their ability to convey a blob of anything that's about the same density as air through space, including things like bad smells, tear gas, or pepper spray. But with these, there is easily as much risk to the launcher as there is to the target.

Meanwhile, I am wondering whether it's possible to launch a ring vertically, laden with a fine flammable powder such as powdered creamer, to form a flaming donut.

Happy vortexing!

**TOP: Tub-thumping a fog vortex at the camera.
BOTTOM: The Boom Stick air cannon connected to the vortex tube.**

For videos of vortex cannons in action, along with more vortex resources, see makezine.com/15/vortex.

THE AMAZING SEEBECK GENERATOR

By Andrew Lewis

FLAME ON

With no moving parts, this simple energy-recycling generator scavenges waste heat from a candle and turns it into usable electricity.

Peltier cells are flat devices that draw heat from one side to the other through a thermoelectric principle called the Peltier effect. The cells are commonly used to pump heat away from CPUs or graphics cards, and are also found in camping coolers and heaters. The Amazing Seebeck Generator uses one of these devices in reverse, to turn a heat differential into electricity, rather than using electricity to produce a heat differential.

I originally made the project because I wanted something like a steam-powered generator, but without the noise and maintenance issues associated with steam. I was pleasantly surprised when I found that my $5, 37-watt Peltier cell from eBay could capture the heat from a single tea candle or alcohol burner and use it to generate about 5 volts at 1 amp, which made it perfect for powering radios, mobile phones, and LED lights. You can make the Amazing Seebeck Generator in less than an hour using mostly scrap or recycled parts, and it has a distinctly steampunk feel to it.

Set up: p.125   Make it: p.126   Use it: p.129

Andrew Lewis is a keen artificer and computer scientist with interests in 3D scanning, computational theory, algorithms, and electronics. A relentless tinkerer, his love of science and technology is second only to his love of all things steampunk.

Photograph by Steve Double

In the Cooler

The Peltier and Seebeck effects exchange temperature differences and electricity. In a thermoelectric cooler, aka Peltier device, alternating slices of different semi-conductor materials connect in a zigzag pattern between 2 plates. Heating one plate drives electrons away in one material while attracting them in the other. This induces an electric current in 1 direction — the Seebeck effect. Conversely, running a voltage across the junction draws heat toward one side while cooling the other — the Peltier effect.

The multiple junctions in the zigzag work in parallel, which multiplies the effects. Whether the device is used to convert a heat differential into voltage, or vice versa, it performs the conversion with no moving parts.

A junction between electron-donor and electron-acceptor materials exhibits the Seebeck and Peltier effects.

Unfortunately, thermoelectric devices are typically only 1%–2% efficient, or 5% with the latest advances. This isn't enough to make large-scale thermoelectric power generation (TEG) practical, although many researchers are trying to raise the efficiency. But thermoelectric generators are useful for other things; they can measure extreme differences in temperature, and are used in heating systems to power convection fans and pumps by using waste heat recovered from stovepipes and boilers.

The principle behind our Amazing Seebeck Generator is simple. We position our Peltier cell horizontally over our tin-can "furnace," heat the underside with a candle or alcohol burner, and cool the topside with a heat sink and fan.

Illustration by Timmy Kucynda

SET UP.

MATERIALS

[A] Circuit board larger than the tin can lid. I used copper-clad PC board, RadioShack #276-1499.

[B] Heat sink preferably a Zalman Flower style, for aesthetic reasons. From an old PC, or about $15 on eBay.

[C] 37W Peltier cell I got mine for $5 on eBay. Search for "thermoelectric cooler" or "TEC" in addition to "Peltier."

[D] 5V fan from an old PC graphics card, about $10 on eBay. CPU fans run at 12V, which is too high.

[E] Tin can with lid The lid must be larger than the Peltier cell.

[F] Bolts, 1" long by about ¼" diameter (2)

[G] Small tension springs, 1" long by ¼" diameter (2) with hook ends that fit snugly over the bolts

[H] Nuts (4) to fit bolts

[I] Alligator leads (2) or mini alligator clips and hook-up wire. You can get 10 clips for $2 on eBay, or $4 from RadioShack (part #270-378).

[NOT SHOWN]
Candle or alcohol/spirit burner

Anchovy tin or other small candleholder

Stiff wire just enough to bend into a small handle

Small metal plate (optional) to seal the opening behind the candle. I used a decorated boiler plate from a model steam engine.

Thermal transfer grease (optional) aka heat sink compound

High-temperature silicone glue or exhaust repair putty

Thin copper wire

OPTIONAL (for chimney)

[J] 90° elbow fitting for ½" copper pipe

[K] ½" copper pipe, (3" OD) 4"–6" long

TOOLS

[L] Utility knife aka box cutter or Stanley knife

[M] Small, strong knife such as a pocketknife

[N] Bullnose pliers

[NOT SHOWN]

Dremel tool with cutting bit (optional)

Drill with bits suitable for sheet metal

Electrical tape or soldering materials

Gloves

Hole saw or circle cutter bit that matches the inside diameter of the tin can. Alternately, you can use a file, but a hole-cutting bit makes it easier.

Marking pen

Multimeter

Wire strippers/cutters

Photography by Andrew Lewis

MAKE IT.

GENERATE YOUR AMAZING SEEBECK GENERATOR

START ⋙

Time: **1 Hour** Complexity: **Easy**

1. MAKE THE CAN FURNACE

1a. Using a small knife or Dremel with a cutting bit, make 3 or 4 U-shaped cuts equally spaced around an empty tin can, near the open end (the bottom of the furnace). Bend the resulting metal tabs 90° into the can to form little brackets. These will hold the can lid later, to make a level platform for the candle.

> ⚠ **CAUTION: Wear gloves to protect your hands when cutting metal.**

1b. Cut another, larger hole in the can between 2 brackets and opposite the can's seam, that extends farther toward the top. The hole needs to be big enough to allow candles and fingers through. Using pliers, bend the edges of these cuts over, into the can, so that no sharp edges are exposed.

1c. Cut 2 more rectangular holes on either side of the can near the closed end (the top), to allow the light to shine out and air to flow in. Drill a hole above each of these, toward the closed end, that's just large enough for the bolts to fit through.

2. ADD THE CHIMNEY (OPTIONAL)

The chimney is not functionally necessary, but it adds a steampunk feel and balances out the design. If you also want to paint the sides of the can, you can use a high-temperature paint, but I prefer the natural shine of the metal.

2a. Drill or cut another hole in the can, near the closed end and through the seam, which is the strongest part of the can. The hole should be the same size as the copper elbow, and should be a tight enough fit to hold the chimney in place.

2b. Fit the pipe elbow through the hole. If it doesn't fit snugly, use high-temperature silicone glue or exhaust repair putty to secure it. Then, fit the chimney pipe onto the pipe elbow.

3. MAKE THE GASKET

You could simply position the Peltier cell between the can and the heat sink, but framing it within a gasket limits the exchange of heat around it, which improves efficiency.

3a. Cut a circle out of circuit board material that's the same diameter as the tin can. You can use a hole saw or a circle cutter if you have one. Otherwise, use a utility knife to cut a hexagonal shape, then file it round to fit. The circuit board is brittle, so score both sides deeply and snap off the excess with pliers.

3b. Cut a hole in the gasket for the Peltier cell to fit into. Draw around the cell with a marker, leaving some extra room for the cable contacts coming out of the cell. Then cut around the outline with a utility knife.

4. PUT IT ALL TOGETHER

4a. Bolt the springs to the top of the can by running each bolt through a spring end, a nut, the can, and the other nut inside the can, in that order. Fixing the depth of the bolt with an extra nut is neater than having a single nut on the inside of the can. Then, attach the heat sink to the 5V fan. I used thin copper wire, but you can also use glue or screws.

4b. Place the gasket on the top of the can, and place the Peltier cell in the gap. To improve efficiency, add a thin layer of thermal transfer grease (also called heat sink compound) to both sides of the cell.

4c. Secure the heat sink on top of the Peltier cell by hooking the tops of the springs to the heat sink's tension bar. If it doesn't have one, drill holes on each side to thread the springs through.

Position the can lid on the brackets inside. If the can is small, fix it to a sturdy base using silicone glue. Then make a candleholder that will fit inside the can. I used an anchovy tin with stiff wire poked through as a handle.

4d. Twist or solder together the red (+) and black (−) leads from the fan and Peltier cell, red to red and black to black, and also connect an alligator lead to each, for connecting the generator to other things.

Decorate as desired (I added a fancy door from a model steam engine to the candleholder), and you're done!

FINISH ☒

FIRE POWER

ONE CANDLEPOWER

Place a candle in the tin can furnace, and wait for the heat to build up. If the candle keeps going out, add more holes to the furnace.

If you've done everything correctly, the fan will begin to spin. If you have a voltage meter, you should start to see a reading soon after the candle is lit. If the fan doesn't spin, check that you don't have the fan wires connected backward.

REGULATING THE VOLTAGE

The output from the Peltier cell is unregulated, and its voltage will vary along with the flame and fuel level. Unregulated power could kill some electronic equipment (although I've powered my MP3 player and radio on unregulated current with no ill effects).

You can rectify this with an LM317 voltage regulator. These cheap, readily available components can be configured to produce a constant voltage between 1.2V and 25V. See makezine.com/15/seebeck for a circuit diagram that shows how to wire a Peltier cell generating approximately 5V to an LM317, to produce a regulated output voltage up to about 3.8V that's tuneable by turning a potentiometer. Output of 3.8V lets you run a high-power LED, charge a PDA or mobile phone, or power a radio or MP3 player.

To power higher-voltage devices, you would need to create a step-up regulator, which combines an oscillator circuit with a voltage multiplier to raise the voltage while lowering the current.

Photograph by Steve Double

! CAUTION: Step-up circuits are moderately complicated, and you should not attempt building one unless you are familiar with electronics, because they can give a nasty (and potentially fatal) shock.

BOOSTING THE POWER OUTPUT

For more power, use an alcohol burner instead of a candle, and raise the flame. Use a smaller can, a larger heat sink, and plenty of heat sink grease.

You can also increase output by connecting multiple Peltier cells together. Connect them in parallel to increase the current, and connect them in series to increase the voltage. Use LN4001 or LN4002 diodes to block current from entering the cells. With parallel cells, connect a diode to each cell's positive lead, with its silver band facing away from the cell. With the cells in series, run a diode from the red wire on each cell to the black wire on the next cell, with the silver band facing black.

Use microchipped wooden tiles to launch your favorite websites and applications.

The iConveyor

BY JOHN EDGAR PARK

■ **I LOVE ANACHRONISTIC INTERFACES.** From steampunk, to clockpunk, to the industrial design of the movie *Brazil*, I'm drawn to rough, tactile designs from another era married to high tech. With the increasingly virtual nature of our lives, I think we ought to enjoy physical interactions while we can, before we evolve into limbless, Bluetooth-embedded craniums. That's why I built the iConveyor, an RFID tag-reading, conveyor belt-driven, USB application launcher (Figure 1).

I have a long, disorganized list of bookmarks in my browser. Recently, while fishing around in an equally disorganized glass jar of screws, springs, and bolts, I thought: Wouldn't it be great to dig around in a tray of application and website tiles looking for just the right program to launch or URL to open? I envisioned using little wooden tiles with icons printed on them, but how would I let my PC know about it? I immediately thought of RFID (radio frequency identification) tags.

I'd never worked with RFID readers and tags before, so I figured this would be a good opportunity to learn about them. Based on the recommendation of a friend who had built an RFID-controlled beer keg, I purchased a Phidget RFID kit (*see MAKE, Volume 06, page 160, for a primer on using a similar kit*).

The kit consists of a Windows/OSX/Linux-compatible USB RFID reader board, some passive 125kHz RFID tags that each have a unique embedded 40-bit read-only identification number, and an SDK (software development kit) that allows you to access and control the board through programming languages such as C, Visual Basic, Java, ActionScript, and others.

I installed the board and checked out the sample software, which displays the unique ID number associated with each RFID tag when you pass it within a few inches of the board. I was able to prototype a Visual Basic program to launch URLs fairly easily, but when my good friend and programmer extraordinaire Usman Muzaffar offered to take over

the software for this project, we switched to the Tcl scripting language (see sidebar on page 134).

I wanted to represent the applications and websites in the real world using small, wooden tiles with 25mm RFID tags stuck on them. After finding out that Scrabble tiles were a bit too small and not perfectly square (who knew?), I got some 1" wooden cubes from an art supply store and cut them into tiles with a miter saw.

I had planned to buy some clear sticker paper, print out icons, and stick them onto the tiles, but was put off by the high cost of laser printer sticker paper.

My frugality was fortunate, because it led to my discovery of a really neat toner transfer trick. I flipped an icon horizontally in Photoshop, printed it on regular white paper in my laser printer, and set it on top of a wooden tile, like a temporary tattoo. Using a 25W soldering iron with the tip removed, I rubbed the back of the paper quickly, with moderate pressure, for about a minute (Figure 2). Lifting the paper revealed a perfect transfer of the toner onto the wood (Figure 3). Awesome! I wouldn't want to do any large-scale work this way, but it worked wonderfully for a small piece.

I stuck my RFID tag to the back of the tile and was ready to go (Figure 4).

By this point, Usman had developed the software to the point where it could read tags and launch applications and URLs. As a test, I edited the Tcl script to map a tile's tag ID to the MAKE website URL. With the RFID reader plugged in, I picked up the tile, waved it over the reader, watched as the website popped up, and set the tile back in its bowl.

Getting this much of it working was great, but something was missing. I wanted more moving parts. More motors. More lights. More switches. I wanted to build a miniature conveyor belt to move my tiles for me.

I took a trip down to my favorite surplus parts store, Luky's Hardware in Burbank. Poking around in the bins, I found four beautiful Bakelite bearing

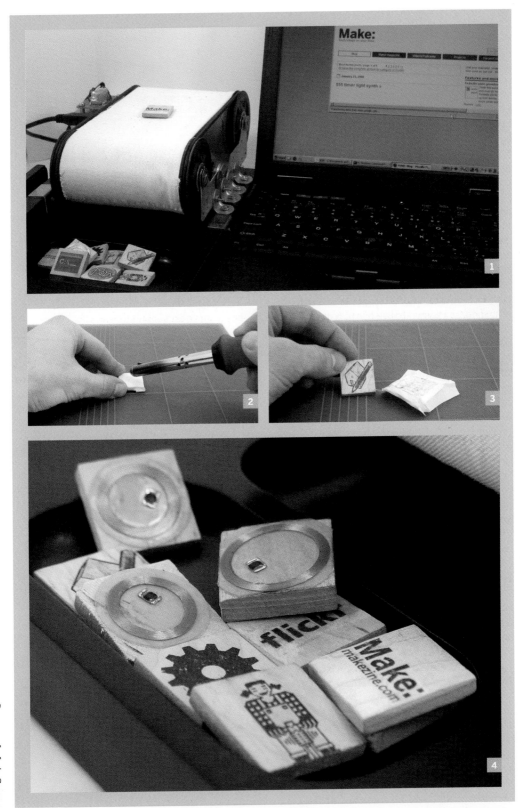

The iConveyor

sleeve pulleys, and rubber O-rings to turn them. After piecing together some brackets, hex stand-offs, and various nuts and bolts on the floor of the hardware store (they're very patient with me) I had the start of a conveyor belt. At home I mounted it on a wooden tray meant for organizing cuff links and pocket change (Figure 5). Sorry, Mom and Dad.

Using a perforated aluminum strip to form a bracket (Figure 6), I mounted the RFID reader inside the conveyor belt (Figures 7 and 8). Tiles dropped on the middle of the belt would be read and then conveyed off the end into a receptacle. I mounted a DC motor to turn the conveyor belt pulley. The RFID board has two 5V DC outputs, drawn from USB power. There are Phidget library calls to turn them on and off, so I figured I'd use one to light an orange LED and one to turn the conveyor belt as each tile was read. Problem was, my DC motor required 12V at greater amperage than the board could supply. I needed a switchable, external power supply. Time to build a 5V relay circuit.

A relay is an electromagnetic switch that can use low voltage to open or close a higher-voltage circuit. I soldered a small 5V relay to a piece of perf board, and added a protection diode across the relay coils to prevent damage to the RFID board from the collapsing magnetic field when the relay closes. I added a resistor-and-LED circuit to the board as well, which would act as a status light (Figure 9, page 135).

Once we got the board sending voltage to the relay, and the relay switching power to my motor, I realized that it was turning too fast. I couldn't fit any gear reduction into the space. My solution was to loosen the tension of the motor on the pulley belt and let the slippage turn the conveyor belt at a slower speed. In the future I'd like to install a gear head motor to slow it down further and add torque.

I cut a cardboard poster tube down to 2 lengths that would fit between my pulley wheels (Figures 12 and 13). These were held in by tension at first, but after they started to wobble I put a strip of double-sided foam tape inside each tube's rim. I stretched a piece of canvas around the tubes to form the belt and then sewed the overlapping ends together (Figure 14). I'm not much of a tailor, but I think it adds a bit of Frankensteinian charm to the proceedings (Figure 15).

On the software side, we chose to keep things

5

6

7

8

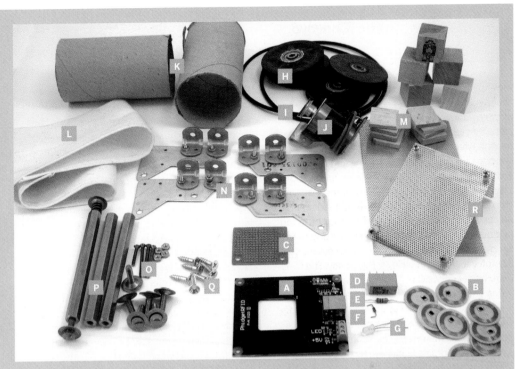

MATERIALS

[A] Phidget RFID reader

[B] 125kHz 25mm adhesive RFID tags

[C] Perf board

[D] 5V DC relay such as Kest #KS2E-M-DC5 from allelectronics.com

[E] 1kΩ resistor

[F] 1N4148 switching diode

[G] 5mm LED

[H] Bearing sleeve pulleys (4)

[I] Pulley belts (2)

[J] 12V DC motor with pulley collet found in many old VCRs

[K] Cardboard poster tube big enough to fit around pulleys

[L] Cotton or canvas material

[M] Wooden tiles could be cut from a yardstick

[N] Brackets

[O] Various nuts and bolts

[P] Hex screw extensions

[Q] Wood screws

[R] Aluminum mesh

[NOT SHOWN] Computer

12V DC power supply

Wooden tray or board

22 AWG hookup wire

Solder

Double-sided foam tape

TOOLS

[NOT SHOWN] Soldering iron

Drill with a starter bit for your wood screws

Diagonal cutters

Small screwdrivers for screwing wires into circuit board connectors

Wire strippers

Needlenose pliers

Large screwdrivers for mounting brackets

Multimeter for testing relay and LED circuits

Sewing needle and thread

Pins for holding fabric in place while sewing

X-Acto knife

DOWNLOADS

» Phidget Library 2.1: makezine.com/go/phidget

» ActiveTcl: activestate. com/store/activetcl/ download

» RFIDTiles.tcl: makezine. com/15/build_notes

simple. Usman wrote the code as a single script, easily editable with any text editor. This includes the mapping of tag ID numbers to the applications and URLs they launch. It means that I can add a new tag to the system just by querying its ID number and copying and pasting it to a new line in the block of code where the bindings are defined (for example: 1300483518 "http://www.makezine.com"). We briefly considered writing a graphical user interface for defining each tag's behavior, and saving the mappings in a separate data file, but it was so easy to hand-edit the data that we decided against it. You can download our script *RFIDtiles.tcl* at makezine. com/15/build_notes.

The script's main launch functions are to initialize the board, turn on the antenna, and wait for tag events. When a tag is read, it's compared to the defined list of known tags. If it's recognized, its application or URL is launched. If not, a console message delivers the bad news.

To prevent accidental duplicate reads of the same tag, the most recent tag ID is ignored for a few seconds. The RFID board's 5V outputs are turned on for 5 seconds, lighting the orange LED and closing the motor relay — long enough to drive the tile off the end of the conveyor belt and into the output tray.

We ran into a few snags along the way. For one, don't try running multiple applications that access the RFID board simultaneously. I had both the Phidget sample application and our Tcl script running at the same time, which caused rapid blinking of the LED and relay outputs. (That's how I found out that nothing is quite so unnerving at 2 in the morning as a relay thrashing open and closed 100 times a second.)

We also began to implement the playing of sound files based on tag reads, but had problems with the Tcl sound extension (Snack) interfering with the voltage outputs. While this incompatibility is probably addressed with newer versions of the library, I decided that I'd prefer to skip the *.wav* files, and add a real-world, solenoid-struck bell in the future.

I get such a kick out of using the iConveyor that I've started to view everything through an anachronistic lens. Could I replace the TiVo remote with an IR-emitting Underwood typewriter? Stay tuned ...

John Edgar Park (jp@jpixl.net) is a character mechanic at Walt Disney Animation Studios, and the DIY Workshop host for the upcoming series *Make:TV*.

TICKLED WITH TCL

BY USMAN MUZAFFAR

From the smörgåsbord of high-level languages available today, including Perl, Python, Java, and VB — some of these already with bindings to the Phidget SDK — why did we choose the Tool Command Language (Tcl)?

First, we wanted something cross-platform. Our example target is MS Windows, but Tcl is also easily migrated to any other operating system.

Second, our program simply hard-codes the RFID constants, but it can be easily extended to have a graphical user interface. Tk is a cross-platform GUI library written for Tcl that's extremely easy to use and flexible.

Finally, the unparalleled elegance of its event model makes Tcl a great match for a project like this. In our application, signals from the RFID reader (events) are being generated asynchronously. Handling this in other languages might force you to write the event loop yourself, or require the use of threads. But Tcl — available everywhere, great UI tool kit, easy event handling — needs only the ability to connect to the Phidget SDK to do the job. That was trivially accomplished on Windows with the Tcom extension that let us connect directly to the Phidget COM interface. On other platforms, it would be easy enough to wrap the Phidget C API with a Tcl layer.

In short, Tcl made it easy to prototype a working solution, and it's a great platform on which to build additional features.

MEET THE iCONVEYOR: The iConveyor is a simple motorized conveyer belt with an RFID (radio frequency identification) reader under the belt. It lets you visit websites or load applications on your computer by simply dropping a chip in the belt. Each wooden chip has an RFID tag attached to it. The reader picks up the unique ID number of the tag and sends the number to your personal computer, through a cable. A computer program written for the iConveyor looks up the name of the website or application assigned to the ID number and loads it.

1+2+3 Two-Cent Wobbler By George W. Hart
Mathematically rich thrills from a cheap toy.

I recently returned home from Japan with some leftover coins and decided to make them into "wobblers." Two orthogonally interlocked disks will roll together with an amusing left-right wiggle. If the spacing between the disks is just right, the wobbler's center of gravity remains at a fixed height so it will wobble down the slightest incline. It is surprisingly addictive to roll these and race them, and you can't beat them as a cheap gift!

NOTE: In some countries it is illegal to damage coins.

1. Cut slots in any 2 identical coins.
With a cutting wheel on a Dremel or other rotary shaft tool, cut a small radial slot in each coin, the same width as the coin's thickness. Hold each coin in a vise while you cut, and wear a mask so you won't breathe in any metal dust.

2. Press the 2 coins together.
Tap them gently with a hammer or apply gentle pressure with a vise. If the slots are not too wide, they'll hold together without any solder or glue.

3. Wiggle your wobbler.
Put the wobbler on a smooth surface and watch it wiggle away.

+ Going Further
After you make a few, you'll want to make mathematically ideal wobblers, in which the center of gravity remains at a constant height as it rolls. For this, the center-to-center distance must be the square root of 2 times the radius ($d=\sqrt{2}r$), so the slot length should be 29% of the radius.

I've since learned of several earlier discoveries of this shape, going back to the mid-1900s, when the designer Paul Schatz used what he called the "Oloid" as part of a paint stirring machine.

Physicist A.T. Stewart first observed that the center of gravity stays at a constant height if the center separation is $\sqrt{2}$ times the radius; see his paper "Two Circle Roller" in *American Journal of Physics*, Volume 34, 1966, pages 166–167. Search the web for "two circle roller" to read more interesting papers about these toys.

George W. Hart is a sculptor and a professor at Stony Brook University. View examples of his work at georgehart.com.

Photography by George W. Hart

THE ARMS OF ASSISTANCE

 Come to grips with this handy vise on a flexible gooseneck. By Collin Cunningham

Circuit board vises are great, but you may find yourself repositioning the head too often trying to get an ideal view of your project. With just a little additional hardware, it's possible to raise a PanaVise Jr. to eye level and free up some valuable bench top real estate.

1. Pick a spot. Mark the holes for the microphone mounting plate on your prospective surface (Figure A, next page).

2. Drill. Make holes with a ⁷⁄₆₄" bit or thereabouts.

3. Secure the base. Send in the screws ... and set 'em straighter than this one (Figure B).

4. Mount the gooseneck. Twist the extension on tightly to ensure a stable connection (Figure C).

MATERIALS

⅝" microphone surface-mount flange
  RadioShack part #33-332
13" gooseneck microphone extension
  RadioShack #33-330
PanaVise Jr. vise head from model 201,
  or stand-alone model 203
Self-tapping screws, size #6 or #8 (3)
Phillips head screwdriver bit
Power drill and ⁷⁄₆₄" drill bit

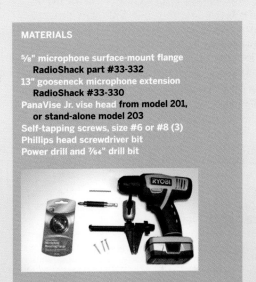

A   B   C

D   E

Fig. A: Mark the mounting plate holes on your surface. Fig. B: Set the screws in straight. Fig. C: Twist the gooseneck on tightly.

Fig. D: Align the other end of the gooseneck with the vise mount clamp, and tighten. Fig. E: Raise your PCB and make a toast.

5. Clamp on the vise head. Here's the hackiest bit. Insert the free gooseneck thread into the loosened vise mount clamp. Straighten the connection by eye and then tighten it up while keeping it aligned (Figure D). It may seem an awkward fit, but don't sweat it — I've found the end result to be quite reliable.

6. Use it! There you go: one arm at the ready, complete with stylish chrome aesthetic (Figure E).

Observe your newfound vertical freedom and visibility! It feels good to liberate that table space for parts, documentation, elbows, etc. I find myself creating far fewer random component piles now.
   Plus, you can now easily raise your PCB to eye level to avoid hideous eye/neck/back strain — healthy!

ONE GOOD ARM DESERVES ANOTHER

Don't let him go lonely. If you've got the budget, add a second arm for concurrent work, testing, and enhanced workspace luxury.

Make: TIPS!

Drilling Perfect Holes
If you really want to drill that hole with *no* tear-out, use a brad point or bullet point drill bit. Then, carefully locate the hole and run the drill at high speed *backward*, until it scuffs down through the first layers of surface wood fibers and burnishes a shallow hole. Then you can proceed to drill in the usual manner without risk of tear-out. —*Frank Joy*

Find more tools-n-tips at makezine.com/tnt.

Collin Cunningham appreciates a good interface — especially those that grant access to audio, art, and electrons. When not building circuits for sound, he can be found blogging circuits for sites (and sights) from Brooklyn, N.Y.

HOLE PATTERN TRANSFER

Prevent hole misalignment in mating parts. By Mose O'Griffin

Illustrations by Tim Lillis

Anyone can stuff a drill bit through a piece of material, but with a little thought and practice, you can develop the skill to produce a hole pattern that allows for accurate mating of parts, to within a few thousandths of an inch (To achieve this level of accuracy, you'll need a drill press; cheap ones can be found for about the same price as a nice battery-operated hand drill.) Follow these guidelines and you'll produce holes that are right where you want them every time.

For this example project, let's say you want to transfer, with precision, a 4-hole pattern, with ¼"-diameter holes, from one ½"-thick steel plate to another.

1. Immobilize the 2 plates.

Clamp the top plate to the bottom plate while transferring the pattern, or find another way to prevent the 2 plates from moving relative to one another, such as setting a heavy object on the top plate.

2. Use a transfer punch to mark the bottom plate.

To accurately transfer the pattern of holes, put a ¼"-diameter transfer punch down each hole you want to duplicate, and tap it with a hammer (Figure A, next page). The little dimple you make under the center of each hole is a very important beginning point.

3. Drill a pilot hole.

Before you start drilling, let's take a closer look at the common drill bit (high-speed steel, 118° point angle, 2-flute, "jobber's length"). Looking straight down the point, the part inside the small circle is called the web (Figure B). This part of the bit does

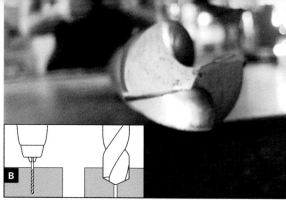

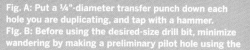

A

B

C

Fig. A: Put a ¼"-diameter transfer punch down each hole you are duplicating, and tap with a hammer. Fig. B: Before using the desired-size drill bit, minimize wandering by making a preliminary pilot hole using the smallest-diameter bit possible. Fig. C: Drill intermediate-sized holes, working up until you get to the size hole you want. It's a perfect match!

no cutting; it forces the base material out of the way so the bit can advance through the plate.

The force of pushing this projected cylinder of material out of the way has the potential to make the bit wander by up to ¼ of the diameter of the bit — depending on how perpendicularly you're pushing the bit in, how rigidly held your work piece is, and how sharp the 2 cutting edges of the bit are, relative to each other. If the position of the hole is critical, as it is in our example, you want to make a preliminary pilot hole using the smallest-diameter bit possible, to minimize the wander (Figure B).

The diameter of the pilot drill bit you select will be a tradeoff between how badly you don't want to break off a tiny drill bit in your part and how accurate you need your hole pattern to be. (A smaller-diameter bit must spin very fast, and is much easier to break.)

The more skilled you become, the easier it will be to drill a hole in a ½" plate with a #60 drill bit. Typically I reach for a #43 bit, because it's neither too big nor too fragile for most jobs, but I have certainly drilled my share of #60 holes when I need a tiny and super-precise pattern.

4. Drill the full-sized hole.

If you're making a very large hole, you may want to drill a few intermediate-sized holes, each serving as a pilot to guide the drilling of the next, until you finally get to the size hole that you want (Figure C).

Use the web diameter to select your size sequence. When the final hole diameter is critical, use a drill bit that's 1 size smaller than the final hole size you want, and carefully clean the hole out with the final size drill bit.

Always use a sharp bit. Dull bits will wander and make sloppy holes. The bit's sharpness can be determined by feeling the edges, and by visual inspection.

Mose O'Griffin is a prototyping engineer with 18 years of machine shop and fabrication experience.

Make:

TIPS !

Tool Protection

I keep a roll of cheap stretch wrap around the shop. It's great for packing away tools that aren't likely to see use any time soon. A quick spray of WD-40 and a cocoon of plastic wrap keep tools and accessories free from dust, rust, and abrasion. —Frank Joy

Find more tools-n-tips at makezine.com/tnt.

Photography by Mose O'Griffin

Photograph by Sam Murphy

PICKUP THE PHONE

 A Les Paul-style guitar pickup from a salvaged cordless phone. By Thomas Arey

We in the maker world stand on the shoulders of giants. Last year I had the opportunity to attend a lecture given by the great guitarist Les Paul.

While he did talk about his music career, in this setting he concentrated on how he came to develop some of his inventions. These included the modern solid-body electric guitar and multitrack recording. It was clear that Paul was not only a true maker in every sense of the word, he was also a true scrounger. His first functional electric guitar was made from a telephone handset microphone and the audio amplification components from a table radio.

I had Paul's use of telephone handsets in mind when my regular trash day scrounging route turned up a pair of well-used cordless telephones.

It was interesting to find both an older 49MHz and a more modern 900MHz phone tossed into the same trash can (Figure A, next page). I was curious to open them up and see what treasures were inside each.

Curiously enough, other than the parts related to RF signal transmission, both units were very similar inside. The circuit boards in both had a fair amount of small surface-mount technology (SMT) parts and proprietary integrated circuits, but there were still dozens of through-hole parts that could fill my parts bins for future projects (Figure B).

After stripping the phones down to their circuit boards, I harvested all the parts I could with my trusty shearcutters. I use Xcelite 170M cutters but any side cutters with blades thin enough to get under the components and still leave enough lead length to work with in the future will do.

The first run-through turned up 7 LEDs, a 4MHz crystal, a 5V voltage regulator, 5 trimmer capacitors, an electret-style microphone, 2 earpiece speakers, 3 antennas, and a fistful of small Phillips-head screws.

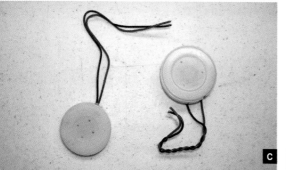

Fig. A: Cordless phones found in a trash can. Fig. B: Searching for recoverable parts inside the rescued telephones.

Fig. C: Could these handset earpiece speakers be repurposed as guitar pickups? Fig. D: An earpiece speaker temporarily attached to an acoustic guitar for testing.

I normally leave components that require desoldering on the board until I turn up a use for them. In this case, an hour or so with a soldering iron will yield another 3 crystals, 25 momentary switches, another electret mic, adjustable coils, and transformers, along with a few small signal transistors. There are also a number of diodes and capacitors well worth harvesting as needed. Each phone base unit also has an RJ11 jack that can be put to future use, as well as standard 2.11mm wall wart jacks.

Inspired by Les Paul, I turned my attention to the handset earpiece speakers from the 2 phones (Figure C). Could these work as guitar pickups?

My first experiment involved connecting one of the mics to a shielded audio cable and ¼" phone plug. I temporarily taped the mic facedown on the soundboard of an acoustic guitar and plugged it into a traditional guitar amplifier (Figure D).

It actually had quite good sound. I experimented further by moving the mic around on the face of the guitar for the best sound pickup and tone. This mic would also work well with the electric Cigar Box Guitar featured in MAKE, Volume 04.

With the earpiece mic properly repurposed, it was not hard to think of ways to amplify the device with scrounged parts. My junk box of recovered radio,

TV, and other electronic gadgets is brimming with transistors and chips that could make a basic amp.

For example, the $5 Cracker Box Amplifier in MAKE, Volume 09, is built around the LM386 audio amplifier chip, a common item in many radios and electronic toys. You could also use the LM380 or the older LM383. The National Semiconductor data sheets for all 3 chips are readily available online at national.com and they include schematics to guide you in the process of building your own amp.

Many other simple circuits supporting these chips can be found on the internet. The nicest thing about recovering one of these chips from an old radio or toy is that the few additional resistors and capacitors needed to bring the chip to life are often found nearby on the same scrounged printed circuit board. If not, keep scrounging! These amplifier chips are like cockroaches in modern electronics.

If you want to go "old school" and you have a few high-gain NPN transistors lying around (common enough in old radios), a simple 2-stage amplifier circuit can be made.

T.J. Arey has been a freelance writer to the radio/electronics hobby world for more than 25 years and is the author of *Radio Monitoring: The How-To Guide*.

Photography by Thomas Arey

MODEL WIND TUNNEL

Getting (or going over) the edge on Pinewood Derby day. By Doug Desrochers

Photograph by Tina Williams

Last year, at the annual Pinewood Derby race for our local Cub Scout pack, we used a Matchbox radar gun (*see MAKE, Volume 10, page 148*) to measure the top speeds of several cars. We learned that they reached 10mph–11mph at the bottom of the slope. Armed with this knowledge, along with some Lexan plastic, a fan, and a precise digital scale, it was time to build a wind tunnel for this year's event.

I wanted to keep all the elements of the tunnel visible, so the Scouts could have fun seeing and learning how it worked. It's a simple, open-loop type of tunnel powered by a household fan at the exhaust end (having the fan blow air into the tunnel would generate too much turbulence).

The highlight of this project is the test stand and its very accurate drag gauge. The stand holds test objects in the middle of the tunnel, and is supported

by 2 hinged struts that pivot backward. When wind pushes against the object, the struts move a back plate that pushes into a force beam, which measures the force. The force beam is hacked out of an inexpensive pocket digital scale that measures down to 0.1 gram.

1. Make the floor and base boards.

I used ⅞" plywood, 8"×40", for the tunnel's floorboard. Paint it to make it smooth. Cut a 3"×7" rectangle out of the center for the test section: first drill pilot holes, then cut it out with a jigsaw.

Make a base the same length as the floorboard but several inches wider, to give extra room for the control panel. I used a 1" board for the base. Line up the boards and trace the 3"×7" hole onto the base — this will help you align the test section later.

MATERIALS

Small electric household fan, about 8"–12"
    preferably strong and multispeed
Lexan panel, 0.220"×30"×36" at some Home
    Depot stores, $34. Similar polycarbonate
    plastics can be found at TAP Plastics,
    tapplastics.com. Acrylic is cheaper, but
    not as easy to cut.
Cen-Tech digital pocket scale Harbor Freight
    Tools part #93543, $15, harborfreight.com
Cabinet handle
Brass hinges, ¾" (2) with screws
Utility hinges, 1½" (4) with screws
Stiff steel wire, 15"-long such as fiberglass
    insulation support wire
Insulated hook-up wire
⅞" plywood pieces, 8"×40" and 12"×40" or
    equivalent in 1×8, 1×12, and/or 1×4 boards
Scrap ¼" plywood and lumber pieces
Wood screws (30)
Wood glue and plastic epoxy
Transparent tape and duct tape
Scrap cardboard or thin plastic
White LED 10 strand (optional) for lighting,
    $2 from IKEA
Box of drinking straws (optional) for flow
    straightener

TOOLS

Drill and drill bits
Screwdrivers
Dremel tool with cutting disks
Jigsaw
Hot glue gun and glue
Wire cutters
Soldering materials

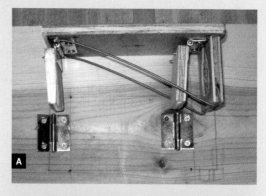

A

B

C

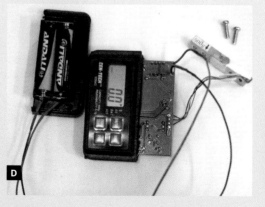

D

2. Build the test stand.

The upper surface of the test stand must be flush
with the floor of the tunnel, and the hinged struts
should pivot easily and balance just aft of vertical.
All other connections must be rigid; minute move-
ments of the stand must be applied to the force
beam rather than absorbed in any joints.

Using scrap ¼" plywood, cut two 2"-square vertical struts and a 2¾"×6½" test section floor. Cut the
back plate 2"×2½" tall, and lighten it with a large
cutout, because weight not centered in the pivoting
mechanism will tend to fall backward and inflate
very small measurements. Glue a ½"×¾" block to
the lower-center-back of the plate; this spacer is
what presses against the force beam.

Mount the underside of the test section floor to
the struts, using two 1½" hinges. Glue the back plate

Photography by Doug Desrochers

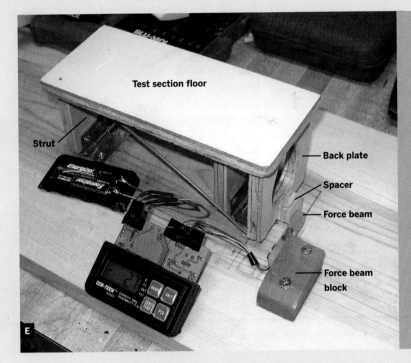

Test section floor

Strut

Back plate

Spacer

Force beam

Force beam block

E

Fig. A: The hinged test stand before attaching to base board.

Fig. B: The test stand balanced to hold the model in measurement position.

Fig. C: The force beam hacked out of a pocket digital scale.

Fig. D: The scale display, force beam, and batteries ready for mounting.

Fig. E: Test stand, force beam, and control panel configuration.

to the aft end, and brace the connection diagonally with stiff steel wire on either side. I looped one end of each wire, screwed it next to the front strut, and bent the other end up to fit into a hole drilled in the bottom end of the back plate (Figure A).

Use 2 more hinges to mount the struts to the base board, making sure the stand pivots smoothly (Figure B). A reliable mechanism requires tight tolerances! I needed a snub Phillips screwdriver to handle these lower hinges.

3. Hack the force beam.

Unscrew the back of the Cen-Tech scale, then remove and save the screws holding the force beam. Carefully cut away the hot glue over the battery and force beam wires, and use wire cutters to cut an opening through the side of the case big enough to pull the beam through, keeping its wires intact. Use a Dremel to cut the frame above the display, not too deep, and toss the excess. Also cut off the battery compartment; I lengthened the power wires for more mounting options and duct-taped them down later for strain relief (Figures C and D).

Cut a wood block about 1"×2"×½" and mount the force beam to this block, using the saved screws. Now, the critical part: lean the stand back slightly

and position the force beam block on the base such that the spacer just touches the force beam near the sticker that says "500g." Hold the block in place, power up the scale, and confirm that it responds correctly before screwing the block to the base board. If the scale reads negative values, flip the beam around (Figure E).

4. Complete the base.

The rest is easy. Cut 4 support blocks sized to lift the floorboard so that its top sits flush with the top of the test stand. I used 2×4 scraps, shaped the middle blocks with a ledge for mounting the control panel, and attached them with wood screws.

5. Build the tunnel and control panel.

Cut 2 pieces of 0.220" Lexan 7"×30" for the tunnel sides, and 1 piece 7⅞"×30" for the top. Cut a test section access door in 1 side. If you're adding LED lighting, the door should clear the floor by about 1".

Mount the door with the brass hinges along the top, and attach the handle at the bottom. Air should not leak in around the door during use, so you need to seal it; clear tape works for low velocities, but Lexan is sturdier and better looking. One lesson

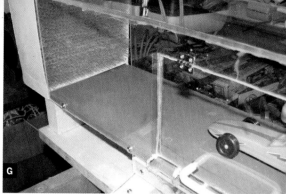

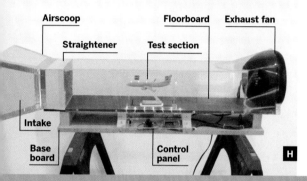

Airscoop Floorboard Exhaust fan

Straightener Test section

Intake

Base board Control panel

Fig. F: Stack 2" drinking straw pieces into the cardboard sleeve to make the air straightener. Fig. G: Air straightener installed at the front of the tunnel.

Fig. H: The wind tunnel with air intake (exhaust fan) and straightener. Fig. I: Testing windspeed with a small anemometer.

learned: glue a small block of Lexan inside the door opening to prevent the door from swinging inward.

Finally, assemble the tunnel by screwing the Lexan sides to the floorboard and using plastic epoxy to secure the top piece.

Below the access door, create a control panel to house the scale display, fan controls, and LED switch. I used Lexan for better visibility. For the LEDs, I hot-glued 7 of the 10 along the floor near the test section and taped the remaining 3 under the test section, to illuminate the tunnel's workings.

6. Mount the fan.

Crack open the fan, extend all its control wires about 2', and remove any unneeded supports. Mount the fan as near as possible to the center of the tunnel, blowing out the back. Seal around it to close any holes between it and the tunnel. I used thin scrap plastic from toy packaging, to preserve the view, but cardboard and duct tape would work fine. Regardless, use tape and hot glue to make the seal complete.

7. Make a flow straightener.

Make a cardboard sleeve with the same cross-section as the tunnel, and pack it with 2" pieces of

drinking straws — this part goes faster with a small-fingered helper (Figures F and G). The straws reduce turbulence, but they also cut the wind speed by several mph, and the tunnel will work without them. To improve performance, add a cardboard airscoop in front of the straightener (Figure H). That's it!

8. Test your car!

Make sure the tunnel is level and stable, for repeatable drag numbers. Tape or block your car wheels on the test section floor.

Now fire up the fan to test your car — the force in the display is very close to the actual drag caused by the car (set it to "grams" for higher resolution). Modify your shape to minimize that drag. Now set track records at the Pinewood Derby!

For airflow visibility, run a Halloween fog generator at the intake and take flash photos to capture the stream lines.

You can measure the wind speed with a mini-anemometer (Figure I) — eBay is a good source.

Doug "Beads" Desrochers (beads27@cox.net) is an aerospace engineer and pilot with ASEC, Inc. He served in the U.S. Navy as a test pilot and test pilot instructor, and has been voiding warranties since early childhood.

FRONT DOOR REMOTE

 Wireless keychain fob controls apartment intercom's door buzzer. By Ryan O'Horo

Now don't tell the co-op board, but I crafted a plan to ditch my Mul-T-Lock key for good. In my apartment building, you use the intercom to remotely unlock the front door for guests and deliveries. I upgraded my pocket keychain to get me into the building's front door wirelessly and keylessly, using a fun $30 RF relay kit from Carl's Electronics. Here's how.

First I opened the intercom panel in my apartment, exposing an unsettling mess of wires leading to its Door, Talk, and Listen buttons (Figure A, next page). The Door button is just a simple, normally open switch, so I used a continuity tester to find its 2 terminals. I stripped the ends of some 2-wire cable, screwed 1 strand to each terminal (Figure B), then closed the intercom panel with the cable running out for access (Figure C). Wiring in parallel like this allows either the relay or the button to open the door.

MATERIALS

2-channel RF relay kit part #HD2COMBO from Carl's Electronics (electronickits.com)**, $30**
12V power supply
2-conductor hookup wire or phone cable
Project enclosure, at least 2½"×3½"×1"
3M Command adhesive tape (optional)

TOOLS

Drill and small bit
Large screwdriver for intercom screws
Small screwdriver for kit terminal screws

Photograph by Sam Murphy

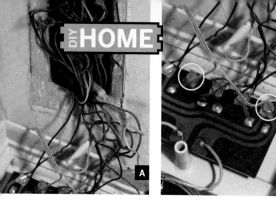

A B C D

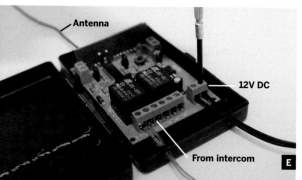

Antenna

12V DC

From intercom

E F

Fig. A: Wires behind the apartment intercom control panel. Fig. B: The terminal screw posts (shown in yellow circles) with my 2-conductor cable (copper/tin) connected to the door button contacts.

Fig. C: Panel replaced with the wire hanging down. Fig. D: Holes for power and door-signal wires drilled in the project box. Fig. E: Connected relay board in the project box. Fig. F: Relay connections and wireless key fob.

OK, time for kit and intercom to meet. The RF relay kit consists of a small printed circuit board that I decided to enclose in a project box. Following the board's layout, I drilled holes for the antenna in one end of the box and for the power and Door wires in the opposite end (Figure D). I put the board inside and connected the Door wires to one of the 2 relays' Normally Open and Common terminals.

I connected the power supply to the relay board's power terminals (Figure E) and performed the learning procedure for the remote, per the included instructions. Finally, I mounted the box on the wall with adhesive tape, with the antenna wire hanging down.

My apartment is on the 2nd floor directly above my building's entry, so range on the transmitter fob (Figure F) is not an issue. I can activate the relay from my bedroom or from in front of the building.

After some experimentation, I found that the remote also works from across the street (about 100' away) and from various places on the 6th floor. It also works from other points behind 4–5 thick, prewar walls or floors, so it seems likely to work from any apartment in the building. And it's a rolling code transmitter, so no, not just anyone with a remote can activate the relay.

And there you go: a keyless entry. I might caution that you not try this at home unless you're very snuggly with your landlord. It's not the most impressive hack, and I want to find a good way to hide the receiver and wire, but it sure makes my life easier.

So, what does the second relay button do? Nothing. At least, not yet.

Ryan O'Horo is 24 years old and lives in Queens, N.Y. He's a web developer professionally, and he also co-founded Make:NYC. Visit his project blog at cravediy.com.

Make: TIPS

Find Your Center
Often enough, I find I want to cut a piece of reasonably uniform wood or other material roughly in half.
Instead of measuring, I use that little trick I learned as a school kid. Just balance it on two fingers and bring your hands together until your fingers touch and the piece balances. It's a quick and easy way to find approximate center. —Frank Joy

Find more tools-n-tips at makezine.com/tnt.

Photography by Ryan O'Horo

EVIL MOUSE PRANK

Control your co-worker's cursor!
By John Edgar Park

Joe Bowers is sneaky, resourceful, and rotten to the core. Whatever you do, don't get in a prank war with him.

Returning to my desk from a coffee break, I sat down, grabbed my mouse, and ... nothing. The cursor was stuck to the left wall of my monitor. I shook my mouse wildly. The cursor moved up and down just fine. But when I jerked my mouse viciously to the right, the cursor nudged a little, then slammed back to its new favorite position, clinging maddeningly to the leftmost pixel.

Blowing on the mouse's nether regions didn't help, so my officemate, Hide Yosumi, took pity on me. "Do you hear something?" he asked knowingly. There was a high-pitched whine coming from behind my workstation. I looked and saw that a strange mouse was plugged in. Not just any mouse. A prank mouse.

Like most analog mice, it once used a ball to drive

MATERIALS

Analog mouse
Tiny DC motor from an old cellphone, tooth-brush, or R/C toy
SPST switch
Insulated 22 AWG stranded wire, 4"
One AAA battery
Electrician's tape
Heat-shrink tubing

TOOLS

Phillips head screwdriver
Sharp knife
Pushpin
Hot glue gun
Soldering iron
Lighter or candle

Photograph by Sam Murphy

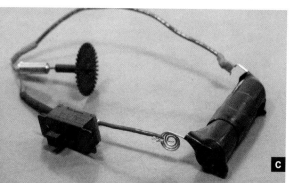

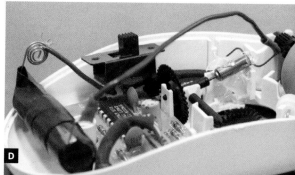

Fig. A: Regular old optomechanical mouse guts.
Fig. B: The rotary encoder disk mated to a motor.
Fig. C: The battery, switch, and motor circuit. Why buy
a battery box when you've got electrician's tape?

Fig. D: Everything in its place, ready to spin the cursor
to the left-hand side.

the shafts of a pair of rotary encoders (disks with notches cut into their edges). Spinning an encoder breaks an IR beam, which drives cursor movement.

Joe had attached a DC motor to the x-axis encoder disk (hence the noise). My confused computer thought someone was sprinting the mouse down an infinitely long table. My attempts to budge the cursor were overwhelmed by this much-harder-working prank mouse. I'm honored to have been so cleverly pranked, Joe.

How It's Done

1. Get an old mouse that uses a ball, rather than an optical sensor. Peel any stickers off the mouse's underbelly, looking for screws. Remove these and pry the mouse open. Remove the ball and save it in your jar of spherical things.

2. Pull a DC motor from an old toothbrush or toy helicopter. Based on the size of your motor, measure where to cut the x-axis encoder shaft, then carefully remove the encoder.

3. Cut the excess shaft off with a knife. Here's the tricky part — mating the encoder shaft to the motor shaft. I "drilled" into the plastic shaft end with a

pin, making a starter hole. Then I heated the metal motor shaft with a lighter until it glowed red, and pressed it into the plastic shaft.

4. I wired my motor to a switch and AAA battery. You could add a variable resistor to adjust cursor speed; a slow drift would be really evil. Joe was pressed for time (he built this prank during lunch, the fiend!) so he seems to have used glittery hot glue for all the fabrication. You should solder and heat-shrink your connections to avoid shorting things out.

5. Snap the encoder in place, then mount the motor to the mouse housing. Taking a cue from Joe, I resorted to hot glue, too.

6. Switch on the motor and plug the mouse into your victim's computer when they aren't looking. Listen for the screams of cursorial frustration to ring through the halls.

Please send any counter-prank ideas my way.

John Edgar Park (jp@jpixl.net) is a character mechanic at Walt Disney Animation Studios and host of the upcoming PBS television series, Make:TV.

Photography by John Edgar Park

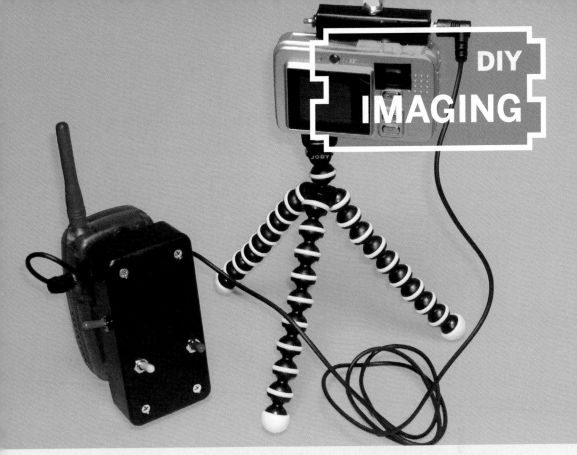

2-MILE CAMERA REMOTE

 Walkie-talkie actuator lets everyone pose without rushing for a timer. By Tom Rodgers

Photography by Tom Rodgers

A few years ago, I was hiking with a friend along the ridge at Crater Lake in Oregon, and I saw a great spot for us to pose for a picture, on a cliff overlooking the lake. Unfortunately, the perfect place from which to take that picture was 250 yards away, over treacherous terrain. There was no way I could cover that distance in the 10 seconds allotted by my camera's timer. So I stayed with the camera and sent my friend ahead to pose on the cliff alone. I was right, it was a great shot, but I was sorry we couldn't both be in it.

This gave me the idea to create a camera remote with enough range to let me take more interesting, adventuresome shots than the standard timer or short-range remote would allow. It occurred to me that a handheld radio could be used as a remote control, enabling me to set up the camera in advance, and then go pose for an "action shot"

anywhere in the camera's field of view. I could then trigger the camera with the radio.

1. Open up the camera.

Open the camera and remove the circuit board; I used a scrap of masking tape to secure the camera's display (Figure A, next page). Find the on/off and shutter buttons on the circuit board.

This camera's buttons consist of a central disk surrounded by an outer ring. A small metal dome sits on the ring, and pushing the button flattens the dome, bringing its center down on the disk, which closes the circuit.

⚠ **CAUTION: Watch out for the camera's flash circuitry; it can give you a shock even after the batteries are removed!**

MATERIALS

Simple digital camera I used a Digital Concepts 3.1 megapixel camera, about $30, but any similar, simple digital camera should work. It should have a fixed or auto focus and zoom, so that it doesn't need to be adjusted when it's first turned on.

Inexpensive FRS radios (2) I used the Kenwood FreeTalk EL, but I've tried to write the instructions so you can use any FRS (Family Radio Service band) radio. Cobra makes a nice inexpensive model that runs about $25/pair. You'll only need to modify 1 radio to interface with the controller, but you'll need a second one to trigger it. If you're careful, you'll still be able to use the radio for standard communication even after you mod it.

⅛" stereo panel-mount audio jacks (2) RadioShack part #274-249

Mini SPST momentary switches (2) One switch is used for the camera's power and the other for the shutter. I had 2 different ones lying around, but you could use 2 from the same RadioShack 4-pack, #275-1547.

Sheet metal such as aluminum flashing, or 0.016"×4"×10" aluminum, Hobbylinc, part #k+s5255, hobbylinc.com

6"×4"×2" project enclosure RadioShack #270-1806

Mini project board RadioShack #276-148

Stereo plugs with wires (2) cut from dollar-store headphones

BASIC Stamp 1 microcontroller $29, Parallax part #BS1-IC, parallax.com

16-pin SIP socket Parallax #450-01601

9-volt battery connector RadioShack #270-324

DPDT submini toggle switch RadioShack #275-614

SPDT and SPST submini toggle switch (optional) RadioShack #275-613 and #275-612

3-pin header Parallax #451-00303

Compact 5V DC/1A SPST reed relays (2) RadioShack #275-232

2N2222 switching transistor RadioShack #276-1617

10kΩ resistor RadioShack #271-1335

Assorted jumper wires

Adhesive rubber feet

9V battery

Scrap of foam block

Paper for making enclosure mock-up

TOOLS

Wire stripper and wire cutters
X-Acto knife
Small screwdriver
Needlenose pliers
Electrical tape
BASIC Stamp 1 serial adapter Parallax #27111, $5
Soldering/desoldering tools
Multimeter
Hot glue gun
Serial cable Parallax #800-00003

2. Test the camera buttons.

The camera's circuit uses pull-down type buttons. When the button is not being pushed, the contact is kept high internally; when the button is pushed, the contact is shorted to ground. This may sound backward, but it makes the camera's circuit more efficient and less susceptible to stray signals.

Set up the multimeter as a continuity tester, and connect one lead to the camera's ground. Then use the other lead to test the button's inner disk and outer ring. For this camera, the meter shows continuity between the inner disk and ground (Figure B). This indicates that connecting the outer ring to ground signals a button push.

3. Mod the camera buttons.

Solder a wire to the outer ring (Figure C). Now the camera will register the on/off button as being pushed when this wire is grounded. Do the same to the shutter button. Put hot glue on each contact to secure the wire.

Finally, solder a third lead to the ground side of the battery pack. Now you can take a picture by shorting the shutter lead to ground (Figure D)!

Discard the on/off and shutter buttons, and reassemble the camera with the 3 leads extending through the shutter button's original hole (Figure E).

4. Add the control jack and new push buttons.

Solder the 3 leads to a stereo jack so that the camera's buttons can be hooked to the controller using a stereo plug. Then solder momentary push buttons between each button lead (on/off and shutter) and ground, so that the camera can still be used by hand (Figure F).

Make a paper mock-up of the custom enclosure, then cut and bend the metal sheet to create the enclosure (Figure G). Cut holes in the enclosure, mount the buttons and jack, and hot-glue the assembly to the camera body (Figure H).

5. Mod the radio's call button with new leads and jack.

The radio mod is similar, but you'll tie in to different parts of the circuit. Remove the cover and find convenient contacts for ground and for the speaker's signal wire, which is usually red (Figure I, page 154). If it's not, just use a continuity tester to find the speaker wire that's not grounded.

Fig. A: Inside the camera, with the on/off button lifted.
Fig. B: The multimeter display shows that the inner disk connects to ground.

Fig. C: Soldering a wire to the on/off button-push contact (outer ring). Fig. D: Touching the shutter lead to ground (blue) takes a photo.

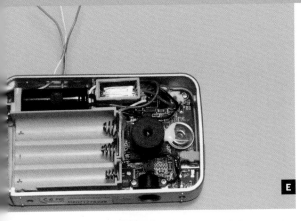 

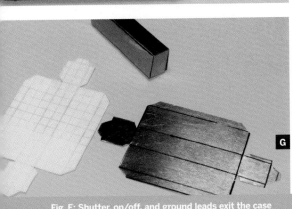 

Fig. E: Shutter, on/off, and ground leads exit the case through the shutter button hole. Fig. F: Outboard buttons let you keep using the camera by hand.

Fig. G: The paper template and cut sheet metal for the add-on control box. Fig. H: The control box glued to the top of the camera.

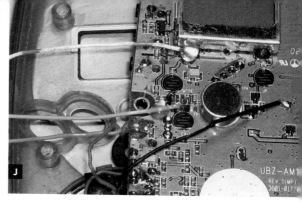

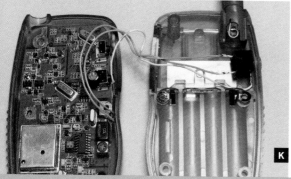

Fig. I: The opened radio, showing the speaker wires.
Fig. J: Radio leads: blue to call button signal, orange to speaker signal, orange/white to ground.

Fig. K: Speaker signal, call signal, and ground leads connect out to the ⅛" stereo jack. Fig. L: The board needs trimming to fit into the controller box.

Find the contacts for the radio's call button (not the push-to-talk switch, but the button that sends the radio's page tone). Solder leads to the ungrounded side of this button, the speaker signal contact, and ground (I took it from the LCD housing). Secure all contacts with glue (Figure J).

Attach the 3 leads to a ⅛" stereo jack, connecting speaker to tip, call to ring, and ground to sleeve (Figure K). Reassemble the radio. If you can't fit the jack inside the radio, glue it to the outside.

6. Assemble the time-delay controller circuit.

Following the schematic (Figure M), mock up the arrangement of the components in the project enclosure, and make holes for the switches and wires. You'll need to trim the project board and the inside of the enclosure to make everything fit (Figure L).

The control circuit is built around a BASIC Stamp microcontroller, which has 8 input/output pins (Figure N). The mini project board holds the parts in place, and wires are used to solder them together. Mount the microcontroller in the SIP socket so that it won't be damaged by the heat of soldering (first trim away the SIP's 2 extra holes).

Using the wires from the radio's stereo plug,

connect the radio's ground to the microcontroller's ground pin (VSS) and to the negative side of the 9V battery, then connect the microcontroller's VIN lead to the positive side of the battery. Connect the VSS, PCO, and PIC pins to the 3-pin header so that you can download the control program to the BASIC Stamp.

Connect P0 (on lead 7) to VDD (+5V) via the 10kΩ resistor, then connect it to the 2N2222 transistor's collector. Connect the transistor's emitter to ground, and its base to the speaker's output signal. When no current flows though the transistor, the resistor holds P0 high. But when the radio's speaker applies a signal to the base, the transistor acts as a short and pulls P0 low.

Connect P1 to the radio's call button so the controller can send an "acknowledge" tone by pulling the call button low. Pins 2 and 3 control relays that can turn the camera on or off and take a picture. Remember to pull the stereo wires through the holes in the enclosure before soldering!

7. Mount the controller and switches in the enclosure box.

After the circuit is assembled, put rubber feet on the bottom of the project board and hot-glue it into the enclosure. Then install the switches (Figure O).

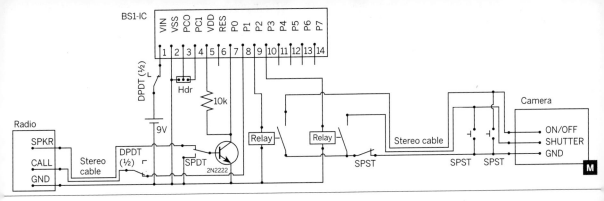

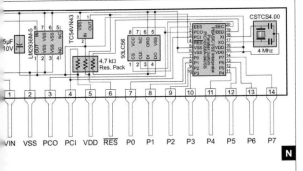

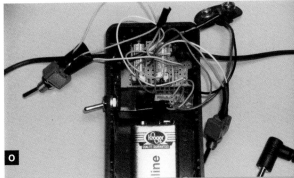

I used a DPDT for the microcontroller's power and to disconnect the radio's call button from P1 when the controller is off. I also used an SPDT switch to disconnect the transistor's base from the speaker, and ground it instead, when I don't want the controller to detect a signal. Then the SPST switch can disconnect the camera's ground from the relays when I don't want the controller to be able to take a picture. These last 2 switches aren't needed, but they can be handy when troubleshooting.

8. Program the microcontroller.

Connect the serial adapter to the 3-pin header (shown at right), and use a BASIC Stamp editor (free at parallax.com) to write and download the microcontroller's code (from makezine.com/15/diy imaging_remote). Be sure that the "<<" symbol on the adapter lines up with the grounded VSS pin. Use a scrap of foam to hold the battery in place, and seal the enclosure.

My radio has a detachable belt clip, which I hot-glued to the enclosure. I added a Gorillapod tripod (see page 151), and I'm all set!

9. Go long!

To take your long-distance self-portrait, aim the camera and turn on the controller and its radio. Then take a second radio, tuned to the same channel, and go get into the frame. When you're in position, press the call button. Once you hear the acknowledgment tone, you'll have about 8 seconds before the picture is taken. A second tone will let you know when the cycle is complete.

If you plan to leave the setup unattended for a while, add a note with an explanation and a phone number, so that no one calls in the bomb squad!

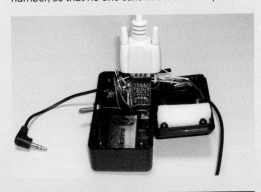

Tom Rodgers is a physics teacher and robotics coach in Virginia Beach, Va. He has been a MAKE subscriber since before the first issue was published.

DSLR TIME-LAPSE TRIGGER

Shutter-control "intervalometer" uses a 555 timer chip. By Chris Thompson

Many digital SLR cameras use ³⁄₃₂" 3-conductor jacks for their remote shutter/focus control ports, which means they accept the same plug that's on cellphone headsets. I used this knowledge to hack a cheap hands-free phone kit into a remote shutter release for my camera, for taking long-exposure HDR (high dynamic range) photos. Later, I found a 555 timer-chip tutorial online and realized how great it would be to automate the shutter to do time-lapse photography.

Then I read Photojojo's (photojojo.com) "Ultimate Guide to Time-Lapse Photography" and learned that the intervalometers most cameras require to trigger their shutters cost $60–$150. I think that's way too expensive for casual experimentation, so I made my own for less than $20.

I'm not too great with designing electronics from scratch, so my friend Michelle Kruvczuk helped

me with the schematic. It's based on a 555 chip, which has 2 input pins that work in tandem: the trigger pin (pin 2) sets the chip's output high when its input becomes low, and the threshold pin (pin 6) sets the output low when its input becomes high. By charging and draining a capacitor connected to these inputs, you can make a 555's output oscillate between low and high.

Add resistors of different values to control how fast the capacitor fills and empties, and you can determine the timing of the cycle. With a variable resistor (potentiometer), you can adjust the timing by turning a knob.

The circuit for this project uses a slow cycle to pause between shutter firings. The current slowly trickle-charges a big 220µF capacitor while lighting the green LED; how slowly is determined by turning the knob on the variable resistor. When the voltage

Photography by Chris Thompson

MATERIALS

555 IC timer chip
Cheap cellphone hands-free headset with ³/₃₂"
   3-conductor plug **This will work for Pentax DSLRs,
   Canon Rebels, and possibly other cameras.**
Resistors: 100kΩ, 470kΩ, 33kΩ, and 1MΩ variable
   (potentiometer)
Capacitors: 220µF, 0.1µF
LEDs: green, red
NPN switching transistor
9V battery and battery clip
On/off switch
Momentary push buttons (2)
Insulated wire
Heat-shrink tubing
8-pin IC holder socket **to let you swap out a bad chip**
Wireless breadboard/protoboard
Small IC PC board **RadioShack part #276-159**
Project box

TOOLS

Wire cutters and strippers
Soldering equipment
Hobby knife and drill

Fig. A: Intervalometer circuit prototyped on bread-board. The potentiometer (upper right) could be shortened and could use a knob.

across the cap surpasses the 555's threshold, it discharges the cap (through pin 7) and outputs a signal (from pin 3) that makes the transistor connect the shutter control to ground, triggering the camera to take a picture. At the same time, the output lights the red LED and, after a slight delay filling a 0.1µF capacitor, signals the chip's trigger pin to switch the output back and start the cycle again.

The circuit also has button switches that let you use the box as a remote shutter release when the power is switched off. We drew the schematic using the free software ExpressSCH (bundled with ExpressPCB, expresspcb.com). You can see the circuit at makezine.com/15/diyimaging_trigger, where you can also download it as a .sch file so you can edit it.

Prototype the Circuit

First you need to expose and identify the wires for the camera plug.

Crack open your headset's microphone, and you should see a tiny board with 3 wires. Cut them free. Camera remotes use 1 wire each for ground, shutter, and focus. Touching shutter to ground snaps a photo, like pushing the shutter button down completely, and touching focus to ground triggers

auto focus and auto exposure, like pushing the button down halfway. Turn your camera on, plug in, and touch pairs of wires together until you know which wire is which; then mark them or write it down.

Before you go and ruin a perfectly good piece of perf board (like I did), build and test your circuit on a solderless breadboard, following the schematic at makezine.com/15/diyimaging_trigger. The headset wires are probably too delicate to push into the breadboard, so you'll need to attach them to some stronger wire.

Test your camera and the breadboarded circuit by shooting some time-lapse sequences. I usually put the camera in position, do the auto focus/auto exposure once, and then set it to manual focus before starting the intervalometer. The auto exposure continues automatically on my Pentax K100D; test yours to ensure the same.

Batteries will work for now, but to capture an entire day you'll want to switch to an AC adapter. With my set of resistors and capacitors, the shutter interval ranged between 30 seconds and 2 minutes (Figure A).

Solder It

Now your circuit can graduate to its own board. I used a mini board from RadioShack that's designed for single-chip projects. Five red wires and 1 black one distribute the power and ground, and otherwise all the components connect via the printed copper traces on the bottom (Figure B, next page).

Before soldering, I drew lines on top of the board to guide my placement of wires and components,

B

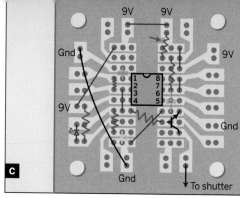

C

9V   9V

Gnd

9V

9V

Gnd

Gnd

To shutter

D

E

Fig. B: The socket plugged into the mini circuit board designed for single-chip projects. Fig. C: Component connections on the underside of the board.

Fig. D: The underside of the board with components soldered. Fig. E: Circuit board, controls, indicators, and other components wired into a project box.

and I made sure everything would fit in the project box. Then I soldered the board and wired everything else (Figures C and D). In addition to the shutter cable, 9 wires run to components off the board: 2 for the power and switch, 3 for the potentiometer, and 4 for the 2 LEDs.

I used heat-shrink tubing to insulate some of these. One additional wire connects the switch to the + side of the power. It gets crowded, so use as little wire as you can (Figure E).

After the wiring, I cut and drilled holes in the box to fit the LEDs, buttons, and pot, and then put everything in place. The board is just stuffed inside the box and the battery case is taped into a corner for easy access. The headset cord exits through a small hole in the side, and I tied a knot in it to keep it anchored.

Converting to Video

Time-lapse video makes it interesting to watch even things like ice melting. Lots of programs, from free downloads to professional video-editing suites, will convert time-lapse stills into video. I tried several of the less expensive options, and had the most success with QuickTime Pro, following the instructions in the Photojojo tutorial.

Limitations

OK, so sometimes you get what you pay for. Commercial intervalometers let you specify an exact interval setting, while this one isn't so accurate. Also, its pulse isn't always enough for my camera to register, so it occasionally fails to trigger, but that doesn't happen often enough to matter much. Someone posted on instructables.com a revised schematic that fixes this problem with a second 555 timer, and a working prototype is on the way.

Meanwhile, I'd also like to figure out how to get the manual focus and shutter buttons to work while the timer is running. Any ideas are welcomed.

See makezine.com/15/diyimaging_trigger for the circuit schematic, links to the Photojojo tutorials and other resources, and sample time-lapse videos produced with the 555 trigger.

Chris Thompson (eagleapex.com) is a 25-year-old digital artist from Philadelphia. His art is generally process-oriented, and he's just now getting into electronics to learn and make something new.

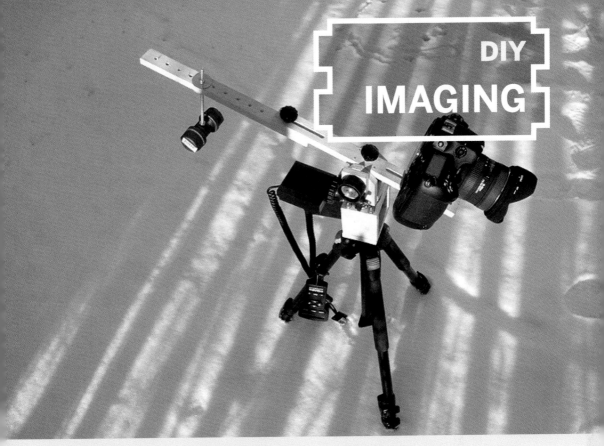

TIME-LAPSE PANNING

 Make ultraslow motion-control camera mounts, on a budget. By Jay Burlage

When I bought my first digital camera years ago, a time-lapse mode was a must; having seen the masterful lapse sequences in *Koyaanisqatsi*, *Microcosmos*, and *The Secret Life of Plants*, I was chomping at the bit to experiment.

After a couple years of experience, I wanted to take my sequences to the next level by introducing camera movement. I knew this required an extremely stable and slow-moving apparatus, and I soon learned that professional solutions had extreme price tags — thousands of dollars. Thus began my quest for a budget solution.

 For a full list of materials and tools for the optional Autostar mount, see makezine.com/15/ diyimaging_panning.

The Right Clock

It all started with a clock. A minute hand turns too fast for time-lapse, but an hour hand's pace is perfect. Unfortunately, most clocks nowadays are plastic-geared wimps, but I found a World War II-era battleship of a clock for just $2 at a local recycle/ reuse center. This plug-in beauty was strong enough to carry and rotate a camera, and its nice boxy design had ample space for modding.

I pulled the hands off the clock's dial cluster and used a hacksaw to trim down the outermost sleeve, which carried the alarm hand. This exposed a good ¼" of hour-hand sleeve to attach something to. At a hardware store, I found a threaded aluminum spacer that almost fit over the sleeve, so I die-cut 10×32 threads around the sleeve so that it would screw snugly into the spacer (Figure A, next page).

Fig. A: The clock mechanism with the aluminum spacer screwed onto the die-cut hour-hand sleeve.

Fig. B: The completed single-shaft clock-based panning camera mount, with rubber feet for tabletop use.

At my local camera store I found the perfect clock-sleeve connector: a ¼" male (standard tripod mount) to ⅜" female screw adapter that had

MATERIALS: 2-AXIS CLOCK DRIVE MOUNT

Sturdy old electric clock
Aluminum spacer, 5/16" OD, 10×32 female threaded or other size to screw onto clock's hour sleeve
Screw adapter, ⅜" female threaded with rubber bumper to ¼" #20 male threaded or other size to connect the aluminum spacer with a standard ¼" tripod mount. Get it from a camera store.
Tripod mount receiver, ¼" #20 female threaded from a camera store
Small rubber feet (4)
Flanged ball bearing, 1⅛" OD, ⅜" ID
Threaded rod 10×32, ⅜" wide, at least 5½"
Nylon washers, 1⅛" OD × ⅛" thick (2)
Steel washers, 1¼" OD (4)
Locknuts for ⅜" threaded rod (6)
Rubber O-ring, 2⅛"

TOOLS

Tap and die set
Small hacksaw or Dremel tool
File
Drill and drill bits

a rubber bumper inside to prevent slippage. I also picked up a tripod receiver to mount to the bottom of the clock. With all these pieces, I could screw the clock onto the tripod, screw the camera onto the clock, and go. I also stuck 4 rubber feet to the clock bottom, for tabletop use (Figure B).

A Second Shaft

The device produced a smooth pan at 15 seconds between exposures, but the camera could only turn clockwise, and slight play in the hour shaft added an occasional wobble. I solved both problems by adding a second shaft to support the camera, which turned via a belt drive that I could cross for reverse rotation.

For the camera shaft, I drilled a 1⅛" hole in the clock face, about 1½" from the dial cluster, in which I mounted a flanged ball bearing. Then I seated a 4¼" length of threaded rod in the bearing with a locknut on each side. For the drive shaft, I screwed a 1" length of the same rod into my aluminum spacer. For pulleys, I sandwiched nylon washers between steel washers, lined them up, and secured them with locknuts. A 2⅛" O-ring served as a drive belt, and could be twisted into a figure 8 for counter-clockwise rotation (Figures C and D).

The 2-shaft setup turned a camera smoothly in

Fig. C: The two-shaft clock mount carrying a camcorder, with the belt reversed for counterclockwise motion. Fig. D: The two-shaft clock mount with the belt in the clockwise configuration. Fig. E: Meade Autostar

Electronic Control kit motors and worm gears installed on a homemade wooden pan/tilt head with an adjustable counterweight (you can also simply attach a camera bracket onto a Meade DS/DSM mount).

2 directions, but the experiment only fueled my desire for more. The clock base was limited to 1 speed, 1 axis of movement, and relatively light cameras; it couldn't support my favorite Nikon D2H and D200 DSLRs, which weigh 3–4lbs with the lens.

The Autostar

For my next step, I investigated stepper motor controllers. The complication and expense of these devices had my head spinning, until I learned about the dual-motor controller kit for Meade Autostar telescopes. Telescope motion controllers compensate for the Earth's rotation by moving very slowly, in a programmable arc, over 2 polar coordinate axes — all of which make them perfect for time-lapse.

The Autostar Dual-Motor Electronic Control (EC) module consists of 2 DC motors with worm gears that you can mount on a pan/tilt head, and a tethered "handbox" remote with a small display. The motors are designed to move a telescope held at its balancing point, so in order to port the kit to my Nikon DSLRs, I built a crane-like head out of wood, with an adjustable counterweight arm (Figure E).

The rig had no problem supporting my Nikons, it was easily portable, and the Meade's 2-axis movement and range of speeds unleashed my creativity.

It ran about $150 for all the hardware and took a good 15 hours to make, but the results were the best I'd seen at a reasonable budget.

Ironically, after I perfected my rig, I discovered that the Meade DS-2000 mount would also work if you simply replace its telescope with a camera bracket. But as they say, the journey is the reward. (The Meade DS-2000 mount has been discontinued, but the DSM-2000 replaces it.)

A friend and I have since developed our own Autostar firmware for any Meade DS/DSM mount. The setup lets you write and run motion-control scripts that "feather" (accelerate or decelerate) a pan and change its direction, all without having to pay tens of thousands of dollars. We're looking for a way to sell our software bundled with the motor controllers, and when that's out, it really will be the ultimate budget solution to time-lapse motion control.

Watch videos from Jay Burlage's time-lapse motion control experiments at makezine.com/15/diyimaging_panning.

Jay Burlage is an architect and a time-lapse fanatic from Ann Arbor, Mich. See his motion-control time-lapse videos and detailed explanations at youtube.com/milapse.

CAUGHT IN THE ACT

 Auto-trigger photos of critters who roam your neighborhood. By Jim Moir and Ken Lange

Ever wonder what's getting into your garage at night, eating your cat food in the backyard, or coming by your tent when you're camping? Now you can find out. With a digital camera, flash, and triggering mechanism, you'll be able to see exactly which critters are prowling at 3 a.m.

Although there are some challenges to overcome, we've discovered that there are plenty of solutions to develop a remote wildlife photography system that meets your needs and budget. Film cameras were used in the past, but clearly digital cameras bring this hobby to a new level by eliminating the expense, time, and effort that comes with film.

What Does It Take to Do This?

Our challenge was to choose a camera system that can stay awake for long periods (most shut

MATERIALS

Digital camera We prefer the Kodak DC-290 and discuss its benefits in this article.
Infrared (IR) detector or motion sensor
Camera flash
Power supply

down after a few minutes to conserve battery power) and to rig a method for sensing the animal and triggering the shutter remotely. We also needed a flash capable of illuminating an area large enough to capture pictures of what tripped the camera. Finally, we needed power reserves big enough to run the camera, the external flash, and the animal-sensing trigger mechanism for several days.

Photography by fox (this page) and Jim Moir (Figure A)

What Camera to Use?

We evaluated the 2 typical camera types — point-and-shoot and SLR — to capture our wildlife images. Both have advantages and disadvantages. Point-and-shoot cameras are inexpensive but need a lot of modifications to work. SLRs have more features but can be pricey.

We chose a third path and used the Kodak DC-290. This modestly priced camera was an excellent choice, with a respectable 3.3-megapixel picture and many programmable features not available in most point-and-shoot cameras. This enabled us to make the system work without extensive hacking, and at the same time kept the total system to a reasonable cost. While this camera is no longer in production, it is regularly available on eBay for $50 to $150 (depending on condition, accessories, and demand).

How We Built It

The construction process was fairly straightforward. We purchased the camera, flash, and infrared sensor, then breadboarded the control and power supply circuits, and assembled the parts into a working system. Go to makezine.com/15/diyimaging_wildlife to download the wildlife camera circuit plan and the scripts that allow the DC-290 to stay awake and trigger remotely.

Now for some of the details:

Stay awake: The DC-290 has a programmable Sleep Time-out function that can be set to a maximum of 18 hours. Given our goal of keeping the camera awake for several days, we added our own stay-awake timer circuit that takes a picture every 13 hours — thus resetting the sleep time and keeping the camera awake indefinitely. We do get a filler picture every 13 hours but clearly this is not a problem when using "digital film."

Triggering the shutter: The DC-290 has an electric triggering feature, allowing the shutter to be triggered without mechanical modification of the camera. We built a pulse generator circuit for the shutter, which converts the signal from the stay-awake timer (or the animal sensor) into an electrical pulse to trigger the camera from either source.

Flash: After struggling unsuccessfully to make the camera's internal flash work adequately, we

Fig. A: The camera, flash, and IR beam setup. For the circuit, go to makezine.com/15/diy imaging_wildlife.

purchased a new Vivitar 285HV external flash for about $90 (it can be bought used for less on eBay). This does a great job of lighting a large area and has several adjustments that provide a variety of lighting options. The DC-290 has the option of using an external flash.

Adequate power reserves: The 4 AA batteries that powered the camera were inadequate as a long-term power supply, so we need to get power from a car battery or 120-volt AC. Our solution was to design and build an external power source capable of keeping the system operating for several days at a time. This can be more complicated than it sounds, because it has to power the camera, electric eye sensor, external flash, and stay-awake timer, which require different voltages, and because efficiency is important to minimize battery drain. Our power supply circuit is shown in the schematic diagram online.

External circuitry required: We housed the power supplies, pulse generator, and stay-awake timer in a water-resistant container underneath the camera and flash platform. The whole rig is designed to be powered by a 12-volt DC source, thus allowing the use of either a 12V car battery or regular house power run through a 120V AC to 12V DC converter.

Connecting to house power is ideal; several 100' extension cords can be connected together to get farther into the woods. If you're out of range of 120V AC power, 12V car batteries work fine, but you have to bring them in for recharging every couple of days.

Fig. B: A precarious meeting of possum and fox.
Fig. C: Raccoons looking for cat food inside the garage.

Fig. D: A startled doe; deer in the headlights.
Fig. E: Two jackrabbits duking it out over the spoils.

How Does It Know When to Take the Picture?

There are two readily available technologies that will sense the presence of an animal to trigger the camera at the proper time.

Motion sensors: Even though these are commonly available and are used in most commercial wildlife cameras, we chose not to go down this path due to their susceptibility to false and inconsistent triggering.

IR detectors: These devices are commonly used in burglar alarm systems, and in the familiar "electric eye" that triggers a sound when a customer enters a store. They use an infrared beam that travels about 30' and reflects off a mirror back to the sensor. When the beam is broken, a solenoid is momentarily tripped, which can be used to fire the shutter.

We found that these work extremely well since they ignore branches moved by the wind and the camera will fire within 1 second of the animal breaking the beam. By centering the beam in the photo, we found that it virtually guarantees getting a good shot of the animal. We used an old RadioShack model 49-310, but similar detectors can be found online for $25 to $50.

Maximizing Results

Whether setting up in your backyard, the open field next door, or a campsite in the woods, look for animal paths or natural narrowing points that would concentrate passing wildlife within the range of the camera and sensor.

Be aware of scents. Move far away from human and pet habitats, as their odors may discourage animals from visiting. Food scraps and animal scents (used by hunters) may lure more wildlife to the camera and keep them there longer so you'll get more pictures.

Endless Entertainment

After 4 years and more than 8,000 pictures, we've accumulated quite a gallery of wildlife pictures, yet the setup continues to provide ongoing entertainment. It's a bit like Christmas when we download the pictures every day or two and find out what was visiting the neighborhood. You may be amazed at what lurks nearby.

Jim Moir and Ken Lange are retired engineers. Jim currently teaches astronomy and engineering, and is a docent at a nature preserve. Ken enjoys riding recumbent bikes and working on his electric Fiero conversion.

MAKER'S CALENDAR
Compiled by William Gurstelle

Our favorite events from around the world.

Maker Faire
Oct. 18–19, Austin, Texas

Yippee-ki-yay, it's Maker Faire done Texas-style! In the second Austin-based event, thousands of Lone Star makers will gather for a weekend of DIY projects, eye-opening demonstrations, seminars, entertainment, and fun.
makerfaire.com

›› SEPTEMBER

›› The B.A. Festival of Science
Sept. 6–11, Liverpool, England
The largest celebration of science and technology in all of Europe, organized by the British Association for the Advancement of Science. the-ba.net

›› Family Day Kite Festival
Sept. 20–21, San Francisco, Calif.
Watch spectacular kites flown high above the Bay. The festival features all manner of kiting, from acrobatic kites to kiteboarding and boating. fdkf.org

›› Sonic Circuits
Sept. 28–Oct. 5, Washington, D.C.
A celebration of noisy extremes where music and art communities can sample experimental electronic music and artistic uses of new technologies.
dc-soniccircuits.org

›› OCTOBER

›› Robodock
Oct. 2–5, Amsterdam, Netherlands
A unique festival creating a spectacular amalgam of science and theater. Robodockers create the entire event on-site, mostly out of scrap metal and other industrial waste. robodock.org

›› The Yankee Steam-Up
Oct. 4, East Greenwich, R.I.
A showcase of all things steampowered, from stationary engines to automobiles to whistles. It's where steampunk makers go for inspiration. newsm.org

›› Space Shuttle *Atlantis* Launch
Oct. 8, Cape Canaveral, Fla.
Seven astronauts fly into space for the fifth and final servicing mission to the Hubble Space Telescope. The crew will maintain the observatory through 2013. kennedyspacecenter.com

›› International iHobby Expo
Oct. 16–19, Rosemont, Ill.
More than 16,000 R/C enthusiasts experience one of the country's largest radio control hobby shows. ihobbyexpo.com

›› NOVEMBER

›› World Championship Punkin Chunkin
Oct. 31–Nov. 2, Bridgeville, Del.
The current record for throwing a pumpkin is over 4,000 feet. Will this be the year someone breaks the mile mark? Hundreds of catapults, air cannons, and other hurling machines compete.
punkinchunkin.com

›› Wonderfest
Nov. 1–2, San Francisco, Calif.
Accomplished researchers discuss and debate compelling questions at the edge of scientific understanding. Watch debates and dialogues about energy, computers, physics, and biology. wonderfest.org

IMPORTANT: All times, dates, locations, and events are subject to change. Verify all information before making plans to attend.

Know an event that should be included? Send it to events@makezine.com. Sorry, it is not possible to list all submitted events in the magazine, but they will be listed online.

If you attend one of these events, please tell us about it at forums.makezine.com.

The Penetrating Magnets Illusion

"Magnets are fascinating things, and they behave in unexpected ways. I will show you a little-known property of magnets, which actually allows them to pass through one another."

» Back in 2004, I invented a physics toy using magnets, one I hadn't seen described elsewhere. So I called it Simanek's Penetrating Magnet Illusion. It obeys Newton's laws, like the others, but why should Newton get all the credit?

This toy is inexpensive and absurdly easy to build. Find a dozen small, flat ceramic magnets, 1" diameter, ¼" thick, with a ⅜" hole in the center. You can get them at RadioShack or hardware stores. You don't need a full dozen, but extras are good to have.

Thread 5 of these magnets, with alternately opposing polarity, on a ¼"-diameter aluminum or plastic curtain rod about 3' long, as in Figure A. You can get the rod at the hardware store. Don't use a steel or iron rod. Plastic is good, but it should be smooth and rigid. A wooden dowel is not as good, unless sanded very smooth, and perhaps varnished. I put rubber washers or corks on the end of the rod, so the magnets won't slide off.

For a magic trick routine, you might begin this way: "Magnets are fascinating things, and they behave in unexpected ways. I will show you a little-known property of magnets, which actually allows them to penetrate through one another — under proper conditions, of course."

Now hold the rod in a horizontal position. Spread out the magnets in the middle, so they're about equally spaced, and jiggle the rod so they find a position they "like." (This spaces them so their magnetic repulsion is just about equal to their sliding friction.) Move the magnet at the left end away from the others, and then with 2 fingers behind it, propel it forcefully toward the others, so it hits with enough speed that you hear at least 1 collision.

Before doing it, say that you're going to make it "pass right through" the others without disturbing their positions. Suggest to the spectators that they watch carefully the positions of the magnets. Now do it.

Your claim seems to have actualized: 1 magnet seems to have gone all the way through, and the rest are in the same positions as before (Figure B). Now say, "Maybe you didn't see that, it happened so quickly." Reverse the action, by taking the one that "passed through" and propelling it back toward the others. Same result: the others don't seem to budge, but everyone hears as it "goes through."

Someone will probably suspect that the magnets just changed positions somehow. So this time, start with the magnets in the center, equally spaced except that you enlarge the spacing between 2 of them. Tell everyone to watch that larger gap. Do it again, and after the magnet passes through, the larger gap is still there, as shown in Figure C.

Yes, you will occasionally crack a magnet, or knock a chip out of one, so have extras on hand. When this happens, just say, "Sometimes, if the atoms aren't all perfectly aligned, they can't quite squeeze through the spaces between them, and one magnet is so stressed that it cracks." After discarding those that chip or break, the remaining ones are probably the sturdiest (survival of the fittest?).

This demo is more fun than the Newton's Cradle toy, and a lot easier to adjust. You do need to

Photograph by Constance Simanek

encourage the audience to watch carefully whether the stationary magnets change position. Tell them to listen to the sound as the magnet collides. People are not normally observant of small details unless told what to look for. A little practice will give you the "feel" for the best starting speed.

When I first played with this toy some years ago, I didn't discover this neat magic trick because I was always being careful to avoid collisions of the magnets, thinking I might break them. So my caution prevented me using a higher speed and discovering how strong the illusion is when done forcefully.

How It Works

The magnets do exchange positions as they collide, but too quickly to observe. Put a bit of colored tape on each one to verify this if you doubt it (Figure D). Each collision and exchange is completed without substantially disturbing the others (this is why we begin with the magnets separated enough that they don't influence each other much). In each collision, the conservation of momentum and energy ensure that the moving magnet stops and the previously stationary magnet achieves the same velocity as the one that collided with it. Then the next collision occurs, and so on, down the line.

This also explains why a larger gap between magnets is preserved, wherever you make the gap, and whichever direction the magnets move. I marked the initial positions of magnets on the rod with a pencil, and found that their final positions are often less than 1 millimeter from the initial positions.

The similarity between this magnet demonstration and the classic toy Newton's Cradle is striking. In this toy, 5 suspended metal balls are initially barely touching. When 1 ball is pulled back and released, it collides and comes to rest, and 1 ball at the other end is propelled away at the same speed as the initial moving ball (Figure E). If 2 balls are pulled back and released, then 2 balls at the other end are propelled away. It works for any number of balls.

How does the system know how many balls to eject? Conservation of momentum and energy are responsible, as well as the fact that the balls have spherical shape, and equal mass and size.

Just because the behavior of my Penetrating Magnets Illusion is something like the classic Newton's Cradle doesn't mean the two are alike. Newton's Cradle doesn't have friction, and its balls do not exchange positions. The magnets do.

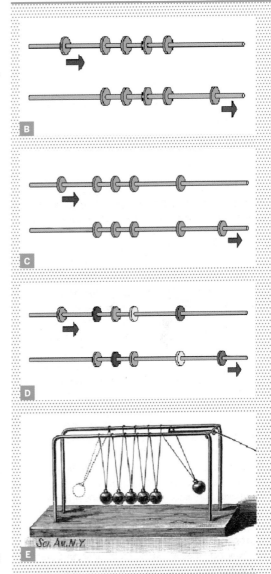

Fig. A: This version of the Penetrating Magnets Illusion uses a plastic curtain rod. The magnets are colored for visibility. Fig. B: The left magnet seems to pass right through the others. Fig. C: The irregular spacing is preserved. Fig. D: Colored magnets show what really happened. Fig. E: An engraving of Newton's Cradle from a 19th century issue of *Scientific American*.

Donald Simanek is emeritus professor of physics at Lock Haven University of Pennsylvania. He writes about science, pseudoscience, and humor at www.lhup.edu/~dsimanek.

Illustrations by Donald Simanek; engraving from *Scientific American*

Handy Tricks from Guatemala

I recently visited Guatemala with my mother, hosted by an amazing NGO (non-governmental organization) called Common Hope (commonhope.org). The oldest archeological evidence of maize cultivation, 3,000-plus years ago, is found here. Many families have been cultivating it ever since. They've come up with some ingenious tricks and tools.

» Monica and her brother Cristobal Jesus (pictured above) guide us up the side of the volcano Agua, near the town of Antigua Guatemala. The trail is steep. People have dug many pits along the trail and at the end of each row of corn beside us. In the rainy season the water runs into these pits instead of washing the trail away.

Monica and her brother are ethnic Maya, like most Guatemalans. And like most families, they grow corn. Corn and beans. The corn depletes the nitrates in the soil. The beans put nitrogen back in with the help of nitrogen-fixing bacteria in the root nodules. Beans supply the diet with amino acids lacking in the corn. The bean vines climb up the cornstalks. It's a perfect system.

The cornstalks grow to 10 feet or more. To harvest the corn, they cut the stalk with a machete overhead. This makes the top fall over so they can reach the ears.

Cornstalk House
Monica and Cristobal live with their family in a traditional Mayan house with walls made from cornstalks (Figure A). The walls are more substantial than you would expect. Handfuls of cornstalks are lashed to a crosspiece with wire. The crosspiece is another bundle of cornstalks. They build fences the same way.

Corncob Tool Handle
Here's a file handle made from a corncob (Figure B). My farm relatives in Illinois also use corncobs for tool handles. A good corncob handle can last a long time and can be very comfortable in the hand.

Ceramic Griddle
Monica makes tortillas on a hot ceramic platter called a *comal* (Figure C). The pat-pat-pat of flattening tortillas is one of the domestic sounds of Guatemala. The family grew the corn for these tortillas right here, halfway up the volcano.

Greasewood Kindling
Their father, Don Filiberto, showed me the pitch-pine sticks he uses to kindle the fire (Figure D).

Tump Line
We met this gentleman named Senso Seis coming down the trail. He's carrying his corn in a net bag with a "tump line" over his forehead, which is their traditional method (Figure E).

Ergonomic Clotheslines
The clotheslines hang down low for ease of hanging clothes. Then long, diagonal poles are used to prop the clotheslines up high out of the way, where they get more sunlight and breeze (no image).

Photography by Tim Anderson

Mule Muzzle Made from Wire

Here are two of Monica and Cristobal's brothers. The wire thing hanging from the tree is a muzzle to keep a mule from biting its passenger (Figure F).

Possum Catcher

Don Filiberto explains how his father used to catch small animals. He'd prop a box or basin up on an avocado pit or another round object. He'd rest a weight such as a board on top of the box (Figure G).

The animal would go inside, tug on some bait, and the box would fall down. Then his father would slide the box around until the animal's tail was poking out and grab it by the tail. I'm not sure what happened after that, but it must have been fun to watch.

Chemical Transformation of Maize

One day I was on a construction crew building a prefab house for a family not far away. The lady of the house, Maria Luisa Garcia, explained how maize is prepared. The chemistry is pretty interesting.

First, mineral lime, aka calcium oxide (*cal* in Spanish), is steeped in water to make alkaline lime water. This lime water is added to a pot of water and used to boil the corn kernels. It makes the endocarp (skin) of the kernels split and come loose. The alkaline solution releases the niacin that's locked up in the kernels. It gives them a nice, nutty flavor and adds a lot of calcium to the diet. I didn't see any sign of osteoporosis in anyone there, even old women.

Then Maria Luisa strains the prepared corn kernels, called *nixtamal*, and rinses off the loose skins (Figure H). If she has chickens or other livestock around, she feeds them the skins. Removing the skins also removes any fungus and associated toxins such as aflatoxin. Then she takes her basin of corn down the street to the miller, who has a power grinder. That's her tortilla dough for the day.

This alkaline reaction process is called *nixtamalization*. It's very important to prepare corn this way. Otherwise maize can't be eaten as a staple.

Ugali in Africa is an example of a maize-based, non-nixtamalized staple food. People who subsist on this without other good sources of niacin get deficiency diseases such as pellagra and kwashiorkor. In some parts of Africa aflatoxicosis occurs, which could be prevented by removing the skins as the Maya do.

Tim Anderson (mit.edu/robot) is the founder of Z Corp. See a hundred more of his projects at instructables.com.

Economic Disequilibrium

Can you have your house and spend it too?

» "What remedy is there if we have too little Money?" asked Sir William Petty (author of *Political Arithmetick* and co-founder of the Royal Society) in his brief *Quantulumcunque Concerning Money* in 1682. His answer, amplified by the founding of the Bank of England in 1694, resonates to this day: "We must erect a Bank, which well computed, doth almost double the Effect of our coined Money: And we have in England Materials for a Bank which shall furnish Stock enough to drive the Trade of the whole Commercial World."

Petty showed that wealth is a function not only of how much money is accumulated, but also of the velocity with which the money is moved around. This led to the realization that money, like information but unlike material objects, can be made to exist in more than one place at a single time.

An early embodiment of this principle, preceding the Bank of England by more than 500 years, were Exchequer tallies — notched wooden sticks issued as receipts for money deposited with the Exchequer for the use of the king. "As a financial instrument and evidence it was at once adaptable, light in weight and small in size, easy to understand and practically incapable of fraud," explained historian Hilary Jenkinson in 1911.

A precise description was given by Alfred Smee, resident surgeon to the Bank of England and the son of the accountant general (as well as the inventor of electroplating, electrical facsimile transmission, digital image compression, an artificial muscle, and other prescient ideas). "The tally-sticks were made of hazel, willow, or alder wood, differing in length according to the sum required to be expressed upon them," he explained.

They were notched to show the amount and inscribed on both sides with the name of the person paying the money along with the date; the stick was then split down the middle so that each side retained a copy of the inscription, and one half of every notch. One part (known as the "stock," thus the origin of this term) remained at the Exchequer and the other part was given to the person depositing their money with the king.

As Smee put it, "Rude and simple as was this very ancient method of keeping accounts, it appears to have been completely effectual in preventing both fraud and forgery for a space of 700 years. No two sticks could be found so exactly similar, as to admit of being identically matched with each other, when split in the coarse manner of cutting tallies; and certainly no alteration of the particulars expressed by the notches and inscription could remain undiscovered when the two parts were again brought together."

Exchequer tallies were ordered replaced in 1782 by an "indented cheque receipt," but the Act of Parliament was to take effect only on the death of the incumbent who, being "vigorous," continued to cut tallies until 1826. "After the further statute of 4 and 5 William IV, the destruction of the official collection of old tallies was ordered," noted Jenkinson. "The imprudent zeal with which this order was carried out caused the fire which destroyed the Houses of Parliament in 1834."

The notches were of various sizes and shapes corresponding to the tallied amount: a 1½" notch for £1,000, a 1" notch for £100, a ½" notch for £20, with smaller notches indicating pounds, shillings, and pence, down to a halfpenny, indicated by a pierced dot. The code was similar to the notches still used to identify the emulsion speed of photographic film in the dark. And the self-authentication achieved by distributing the information across two halves of a unique piece of wood is analogous to the way large numbers, split into two prime factors, are used to authenticate digital financial instruments today.

So far, so good. The breakthrough was in money being duplicated: the King gathered real gold and silver into the treasury through the Exchequer, with the tally given in return attesting to the credit of the holder, who could enter into trade, manufacturing, or other ventures, eventually producing real wealth

Aren't we just passing around digital versions of the tallies we've been using for almost 1,000 years?

Photograph courtesy of the National Archives UK: transcription at makezine.com/go/tallystick

And in the beginning, there were tally sticks. This collection of 13th-century Exchequer "stocks" is stored at the National Archives in London.

with nothing more than a notched wooden stick. So what's the problem? Aren't we just passing around digital versions of the tallies we've been using for almost 1,000 years? Aren't mortgages, whether prime or subprime, just a modern version of paying for houses with fraud-resistant sticks?

The roots of the current financial meltdown can be found in John von Neumann's model of general economic equilibrium, first developed in 1932. Von Neumann elucidated the behavior of an expanding, autocatalytic economy where "goods are produced not only from 'natural factors of production,' but ... from each other," and he proved the coexistence of equilibrium and expansion using the saddle-point topology of convex sets.

Some of his assumptions — such as "the natural factors of production, including labour, can be expanded in unlimited quantities" and that "all income in excess of necessities of life will be reinvested" — appeared unrealistic to others at the time, less so now that Moore's Law and the zero-cost replication of information are driving today's economy. Other assumptions, like an invariant financial clock cycle, are conservative under the conditions now in play.

Von Neumann, who made seminal contributions to digital computing, left a number of distinct monuments to his abbreviated career, among them his *Theory of Games and Economic Behavior* (with Oskar Morgenstern) and his *Theory of Self-Reproducing Automata* (with Arthur Burks). Synthesis between these 2 regimes is now advancing so quickly that no unified theory of the economics of self-reproducing systems has been able to keep up. Periodic instability should come as no surprise. We may be on the surface of a balloon. Or in the saddle of a dynamic equilibrium — we hope.

The unlimited replication of information is generally a public good (however strongly music publishers and software developers disagree). The problem starts, as the current crisis demonstrates, when unregulated replication is applied to money itself. Highly complex

computer-generated financial instruments (known as derivatives) are being produced, not from natural factors of production or from other goods, but purely from other financial instruments.

When the Exchequer splits the tally stick in two, the king keeps the gold, and you keep one half of the stick. Derivatives are the equivalent of splitting off (and selling) further copies of the same stick — or the "clipping" and debasing of coinage that led Isaac Newton to spend the later part of his life reforming the financial system as master of the Royal Mint.

The result is a game of musical chairs that follows von Neumann's model of an expanding economic equilibrium — until the music stops, or we bring in Isaac Newton, whichever comes first.

George Dyson, a kayak designer and historian of technology, is the author of *Baidarka*, *Project Orion*, and *Darwin Among the Machines*.

Binoculars for beginners, über-accurate torque, a tea-serving robot, and 100 monsters.

TOOLBOX

Making Waves
SOS Guitar Tuner
$15 planetwaves.com

When I saw an ad in *Rolling Stone* for the Planet Waves SOS guitar tuner, I knew I had to get my hands on one. Unlike traditional tuners, which are microphone-based, the SOS uses two flashing LEDs to determine the correct vibration of each string visually. Cooler still, the gadget is merely the size of a large guitar pick and sells for only 15 bucks.

Using the tuner is easy but unusual. To tune a string, set the dial to the correct note. Place the tuner above the string with the LEDs pointing downward and pluck the string. The LEDs begin flashing, corresponding to the vibrations of the string. Slowly twist the tuning peg until the lights stop flashing. Voilà. Your string is in perfect tune!

The SOS is light, portable, cheap, and stylish. Best of all, because it senses the string vibrations visually, it can tune a guitar in a loud room, or even during a gig, where a traditional tuner would be overcome by background noise. It took a little getting used to, but after a few strums of my perfectly tuned guitar, this tuner became one of my best new musical friends.

—*Justin Morris*

H₂On

Firefly Lantern Bottle Lid

$22 guyotdesigns.com

An outdoorsman's two best friends are his flashlight and his water bottle, so wouldn't it be great if the two could be combined?

The Firefly by Guyot Designs does just that. Built-in LEDs on the inside of this replaceable lid illuminate your transparent, wide-mouth bottle when activated, transforming it into a portable lantern. It can also be used as a directional beam, making it a worthwhile piece of equipment that I highly recommend.

—*Alex Sugg*

Mag-Blok

$27–$40 benchcrafted.com

This thing goes way beyond the average magnetic kitchen knife strip. Instead of a couple of metal strips that may ding and scratch, there is only wood to touch my beloved tools. The Mag-Blok looks like a single block of wood, thanks to its nearly invisible seam where the magnets are hidden inside. Installation is simple — just drill anchors for the two provided brass screws, then screw them through the countersunk mounts.

The magnets inside are pretty darned strong. Even living in earthquake-prone Southern California, I have no worries about my tools falling. Now I hang wire cutters, a flashlight, X-Acto knife, wire stripper, screwdrivers, pliers, and more. For my home office project area, this is a great way to stay organized.

—*John Edgar Park*

Tri-Bot

$100 wowwee.com

Tri-Bot caught my eye because each wheel has ten free-turning rollers perpendicular to the rotational axis, so a wheel can glide sideways while the other two turn. Tri-Bot can navigate tight, cluttered quarters that traditional robots can only dream of.

He's got IR sensors to prevent him from bumping into walls, although they're mounted too high in his chest to see some obstacles, like shoes and cats. In free-roaming mode, he's like a wisecracking Roomba.

As with many robot toys, the novelty can wear off quickly; I'm already scheming about hacking him. There's a rich history of modifying WowWee's Robosapien, so I can't wait to see what people will do with the Tri-Bot. Highly mobile wi-fi stun gun, anyone?

—*John Edgar Park*

Making Fun from Scratch

Scratch software
Free scratch.mit.edu

ROBOTS

Ashley and her shed-built robot. I conclude: Use Scratch to get a lot of kids comfortable with programming, then use Mindstorms to go deep for those who are interested.

For the past two years I've taught a computer club at my local primary school. I get six or eight kids aged 8–10 for two hours at a time, once a week for three or four weeks. They vary in previous experience from "play computer games all the time" to "Mum doesn't believe in computers." This year I believe I had a big success — I got the kids programming and loving it.

The first year, I'd tried the Lego Mindstorms NXT kit, but it wasn't a straightforward win. On the positive side, the graphical programming environment worked well. The kids were able to grasp loops and conditions and so on, without having to struggle with parentheses or indents.

Against that, though, we ran into several significant problems. The hardware isn't high enough quality — tracking a line across a sheet of paper sounds like a great project but the light sensor wasn't able to reliably do the job. Kids need strong positive feedback when they get it right, otherwise they rapidly lose interest. They like the idea of a robot, but they're not so excited by the reality of it.

I had much more success with Scratch, a graphical programming environment out of MIT. The kids got quick successes from moving drawings and bouncing them off the sides. They learned the same concepts I was teaching with the Mindstorms kit, but Scratch had more things they could relate to. They were constantly calling each other over to say "look at what I did!"

One girl, whose parents firmly don't want a computer at home, built an animated summary of the first chapter of her favorite book. (Golden rule of teaching kids: give them the tools and let them build what they want — they'll fight to keep the laptop if they're doing

something around their interests.)

I think there's a lesson here: doing something in hardware isn't automatically cool, particularly for kids. Adults think that because it's physical, real, and a *robot*, kids will automatically be excited. But for kids who are learning, and who don't appreciate the significance of the challenge, it's just hard and unrewarding.

It's not all bad news for robots, though. I had one 10-year-old girl, Ashley, who loved it and wanted more. I gave her an old original Mindstorms kit, and she's been building robots ever since. Her parents say she's vanished into the shed where the computer is and they haven't seen her after school for a week. I conclude: Use Scratch to get a lot of kids comfortable with programming, then use Mindstorms to go deep for those who are interested.

—Nat Torkington

ProdMod LED Hula Hoop Kit

$50 Product code MKPM2

Dance in the dark with your own homemade LED hula hoop. No resistors or soldering required!

Karakuri Tea-Serving Robot Kit

$65 Product code MKGK6

Based on a mechanical doll manual from 1796, this tea-serving Karakuri "robot" harkens back to the Edo period of Japan.

Herbie the Mousebot Kit

$40 Product code SBMSY

Perfect for beginners, this little light-chasing robot will have you chasing after it. We found that out the hard way when one got loose in the warehouse!

« Untangling Innovation

Jacquard's Web: How a Hand Loom Led to the Birth of the Information Age
by James Essinger $19 Oxford University Press

As the age-old link between craft and technology takes on new life, author James Essinger does a delightful job of unraveling innovations, through many twists and turns of fate, to their various origins. A silkworm in a cup of tea spawns a textile empire in China, royal hairdressers recently unemployed by the French Revolution labor in one of the earliest examples of modern data entry, and, most significantly here, the age of computing is traced back to its beginning.

Essinger leads us back, through the early days at IBM, the U.S. census of 1880, and Lady Ada Byron Lovelace, to an unlikely source: a punch-card-operated weaving loom. Full of intrigue, historical detail, and unusual perspective on the fates of technologies, *Jacquard's Web* provides surprising insight into what actually makes innovation stick. —*Meara O'Reilly*

« Monster Mash

100 Days of Monsters **by Stefan G. Bucher**
$20 HOW Books

The beautiful result of a compellingly obsessive project, *100 Days of Monsters* chronicles designer, illustrator, and author Stefan Bucher's creation of a monster every day for 100 straight days. Each one born from a random inkblot on a page, Bucher drew the elaborate creatures and filmed them in the process, posting the movies to his website, dailymonster.com. The monsters quickly took on lives of their own as an equally obsessive, worldwide community of visitors contributed imaginary stories about each one.

At the end of the project, Bucher was inspired to create this multifaceted book and DVD, sharing his charming wit and passion for whimsical illustration, including more than 250 user-generated stories, 100 drawings, and a few funny info-graphics. It's an entertaining and inspired read, and the movies and bonus "open source ink blots" are a great time-sucker. —*Daniel Carter*

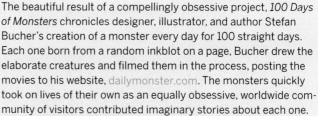

« Building Blocks

Woodworking **by John Kelsey**
$13 Fox Chapel Publishing

Long ago, my parents enrolled me in a kids' woodworking class, and it was transformative for this bookish little girl. Not everyone has access to such a class anymore (or a parent who knows their way around a shop), but this book just might fill the gap.

It starts out with a great primer on wood, tools, and materials. The projects are basic but fun, perfect for a kid learning how to use a saw and miter box. They start out easy but progress through a toolbox, a block racer, a bookshelf, and a rubber-band paddle boat (I still have the one I built years ago!). —*Arwen O'Reilly Griffith*

As chosen by Terrie Miller of Citizen Science Projects

**Nikon
Action Series**

Nikon Monarch Series

Eagle Optics Ranger Series

Swarovski EL

I love showing someone a bird or animal through my binoculars. Their first reaction is surprise and wonder at the detailed view of the animal. Their second reaction is to pull the binoculars down and look at them: "What kind of binoculars are these?!"

The truth is, any decent binoculars will open the door to entrancing views of wildlife, but buying them is fraught with details. What if you just want a pair to get started, without learning every detail? I'm going to go out on a limb here and make specific recommendations.

Binocular sizes are indicated by two numbers: the *magnification* and the *diameter* of the objective lens, in millimeters. Ignore any models that claim to be "zoom" lenses. They're more trouble than they're worth, and you'll probably have a harder time getting a good crisp focus with them.

» For birding and wildlife get 8×42 or 10×42. (If you're a beginner, get 8×42; if you'll mostly be looking at faraway critters, get 10×42.)

» For fast-moving subjects, sporting events, twilight conditions, or just general-purpose viewing, get 7×50. Not every model is available in this size, but it's a great one to consider for beginners.

» Astronomers, choose 10×50. If you'll be looking at stationary objects like planets, they're great for a little boost in magnification and light-gathering power.

If you're on a tight budget, I recommend the Nikon Action series, at less than $100. (I don't recommend you buy anything cheaper than this.) They have good optics in a sturdy package. The Nikon Action ATB series is a little more expensive and better for more rugged use.

For a mid-range budget, I suggest Nikon Monarchs at about $300, or Eagle Optics Rangers at about $320. My current binoculars are Eagle Optics 8×42s, and I love them. I broke the eye cups on mine after a couple of years of hard, almost daily use, but the fine folks at Eagle Optics recently repaired them, for no charge, and sent them back to me in a jiffy.

If money is no object, don't mess around — get yourself a pair of Swarovski EL or SLC binoculars. They'll cost you a grand or two, but you'll have people like me drooling over your optics, and your views will be outstanding.

It's best if you can try out binoculars in person, but an online dealer with a solid return policy is also good. Local nature and birding stores and outdoor retailers like REI will carry some of these brands. If you want to order online, I highly recommend Eagle Optics.

Good luck! Soon you'll be sharing those "wow!" moments with others. And I'll bet it won't be long before you hear, "What kind of binoculars are these?!"

Terrie Miller is a hawk watcher and birder in Northern California, and writes about citizen science projects at citizensci.com. For more binoculars resources and tips, visit citizensci.com/?p=100.

Make Memories ColorPad Journal

$5 makezine.com/go/colorpad

ColorPad

Life in the '50s

When I found out that 60% of nursing home residents will never receive a visit, I wanted to do something. I don't sing or play an instrument, so I was nervous about what I would do or talk about.

I took a ColorPad, a combined coloring book and memory journal, and I didn't have to worry. ColorPad comes in three decades, the 50s, 60s, and 70s. The pictures and the memory prompts on the journal pages sparked plenty of talk.

I'm not sure how, but a discussion of a microwave picture led to one lady's story of a dog eating her husband's dentures and we all laughed. One resident even said, "I don't want ice cream. What I want is to color." I found out later that not much takes precedence over ice cream.

Another lady said she couldn't remember anything. But as she paged through the ColorPad, she began a childhood recollection of living in a log cabin. She added a bit more to the story every few minutes until she had a complete memory. ColorPad also created a pleasant memory for me. I look forward to visiting again. —Carol Scott

Drain Maintainer

$9 terracycle.net

I hate standing in a puddle of water while I shower. I also hate super toxic cleaners, so I've resorted to pouring boiling water down the drain, mixing up vinegar and baking soda cocktails, and just plain cursing.

Enter Terracycle's Drain Maintainer and Cleaner. While it doesn't work on a seriously stopped pipe (for that, see our review at makezine.com/pub/tool/kleer_drain), it works slow magic on reluctant drains.

Following the instructions on the label, I splashed a generous amount of the cleaner into my drain each morning after my shower, and by the fifth day, I could see the light at the end of the tunnel. (OK, not literally.)

With their expanding line of eco-friendly home, school, office, and garden supplies (I really love their orchid fertilizer), plus an awesome packaging recycling program, Terracycle is really doing their bit to "eliminate the idea of waste." Sold online or at Walgreens, Wal-Mart, Home Depot, Orchard Supply, Whole Foods, and Target stores. —AG

Tricks of the Trade By Tim Lillis

Tame your tangles before you melt their faces.

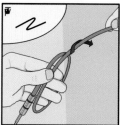

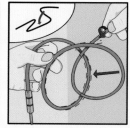

Tangled cables? Try this trick, shared by Adam Carson from the band Microfiche, to keep your cables neat and ready to spring out tangle-free.

Begin with one end in your hand, facing toward you. Start wrapping the cable in a clockwise motion, twisting it about 180° away from you as you complete the loop.

As you make the next loop, twist the cable again, this time 180° toward you. Tuck that loop in between the 2 parts of the first loop, and continue alternating the 2 steps until the cable is coiled.

When it's time to use the cable, simply hold one end and toss the other. Watch your cable uncoil gracefully and without tangles.

Have a trick of the trade? Send it to tricks@makezine.com.

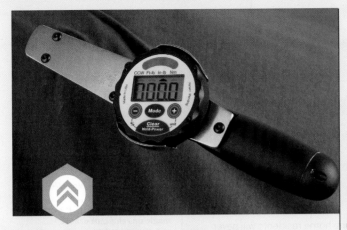

Jetco Digital Torque Wrench

$300 and up itorque.com/Electronicwrenches.htm

Of all the ways to fasten objects, threaded fasteners are probably the most common and effective. But so much trickery lies inside: designers must consider temperature, material, size and pitch of the fastener, number of threads engaged, type of loading, and on and on. Knowing all this, how does one accurately control the joint?

With an accurate torque wrench, of course, calibrated to within 1% of indicated torque! The Jetco ED-50F wrench meets these needs with a digital meter indicating the real-time torque on the fastener, three LEDs that light in stages as you approach your pre-programmed torque limit, and a buzzer that lets you know when you've exceeded your torque setting. With more options like peak hold and RS-232 data output, this wrench is the duck's guts when it comes to accurately tightening fasteners.   —*Luigi Oldani*

The Really Universal Remote

$250 logitech.com

The Logitech Harmony One is unlike any universal remote you've ever used. It does away with the large touchscreen and adds buttons that not only make it more functional than its predecessor, but incredibly easy to use whether day or night.

Harmony remotes are unique in that they can control just about anything. After installing the program on your Mac or PC, you need only to connect the remote to the computer and tell it what products you want it to work with: TVs, music and video systems, game consoles, and thousands of home appliances. From there, you can choose the devices with the remote's touchscreen and control every device in the house. You'll quickly find it's well worth the cost of admission.   —*Don Reisinger*

Magnetic Belt Clip

$13 magnogrip.com

I've always liked those magnetic dishes that some mechanics have on their toolboxes to hold metal odds and ends, but MagnoGrip is even better. It sticks on you! The belt clip is perfect for those little metal components that are easy to misplace.

It takes a little while to get used to; the first hour or so, I kept forgetting where I'd put things, only to find them attached to my belt clip. The magnet is so strong, I stuck a file on there and it didn't budge.

MagnoGrip also makes magnetic suspenders, tool belts, and wristbands, so you never need to lose anything again (but don't get too close to your computer). Plus wearing one of these, you'll get serious geek points.   —*Kris Magri*

Tim Lillis is a jack of all trades, master of none — except for illustration.

Kris Magri is an engineering intern at MAKE who gets serious geek points.

Justin Morris is an avid guitarist and aspiring technophile.

Luigi Oldani is a mechanical engineer in Oakland, Calif., who believes strongly in accurately torqued fasteners.

Meara O'Reilly is an intern at CRAFT.

John Edgar Park works at Walt Disney Animation Studios and hosts the upcoming series *Make:TV*.

Don Reisinger is a popular technology columnist. Check out what he's up to on twitter.com/donreisinger.

Carol Scott has seven grown children and collects pictures drawn by her 15 beautiful grandchildren.

Alex Sugg is an outdoor enthusiast from Winston-Salem, N.C.

Nat Torkington's kids love to ask him, "What did the dinosaurs program in when you were a boy, Daddy?"

Have you used something worth keeping in your toolbox? Let us know at toolbox@makezine.com.

MAKE's favorite puzzles. (When you're ready to check your answers, visit makezine.com/15/aha.)

Festival Lineup

A music festival was held last week for 4 days, with 1 show each night at a different time between 8:30 and 8:50. Each of the 4 performers played their favorite instrument, for 1 night only.

Ted did not play the violin. The Thursday show started at 8:30, but Brett did not perform. Jason, who doesn't play the flute, starred in a time slot that was 5 minutes later than the person who played the piano. The Sunday show featured a flute. The 8:40 show was not the Friday show. Brett did not play the Saturday show. Dan played on Friday, but did not play the piano. The 8:50 show featured a guitar.

Who played what and when?

Russian Roulette

After sending competing assassins to each other's castles, the evil king and the evil queen decide to settle their differences face to face. The king proposes a game of Russian roulette, and the queen accepts. The king then places 2 bullets in 2 consecutive chambers of the 6-chamber revolver and gives the cylinder a spin. He points the gun at himself and pulls the trigger ... click! He hands the gun to the queen and says, "You can give it another spin if you want, or you can just pull the trigger." What does the queen's sage advise her to do?

Michael Pryor is the co-founder and president of Fog Creek Software. He runs a technical interview site at techinterview.org.

Illustrations by Roy Doty

Brain-Friendly Learning

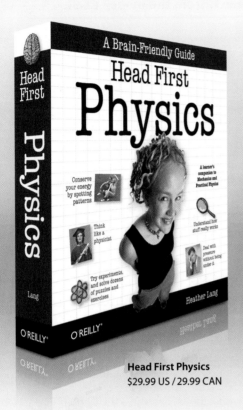

Head First Physics
$29.99 US / 29.99 CAN

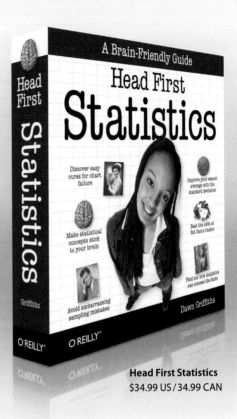

Head First Statistics
$34.99 US / 34.99 CAN

Learning doesn't just happen to you.
It's something you do.

With Head First, it's also pretty interesting—in fact, we guarantee you'll be more engaged and will learn just about anything more quickly the Head First way. Even when you're tackling the hard stuff, like physics and statistics.

Dive into *Head First Physics* and *Head First Statistics* and see how much fun learning these topics can be, even if you're one of those people who "just don't get it." You'll soon be so deep into happily exploring the mechanics of physics and the intricacies of statistical histograms, probability distributions, and chi square analysis, you'll wonder why you ever thought these subjects were hard to learn.

Now for Math and Science from Head First

www.headfirstlabs.com

O'REILLY

Mouse Trap
By Tom Parker

Sometimes it costs more to buy it than to make it from the money itself.

$29.99

Live Mouse Trap

↑ $0.82

Penny Mouse Trap

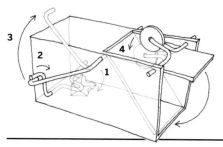

THE MONEY TRAP: The trap is a box with a swinging door. A lever (3) holds the door open. The door lever is held by a bait wire (1), which has a little arm (2) extending to the outside. When the mouse touches the bait it rotates the arm, which releases the door lever. The weight of the door causes it to swing down and shut. The penny and wire on top of the door (4) are a locking mechanism so the mouse can't get back out. When the door swings down, the penny on the wire rolls downward to about a 45° angle, thereby wedging the door shut with the mouse inside. *Eeeek! It's a trap!*

Photograph and illustration by Tom Parker

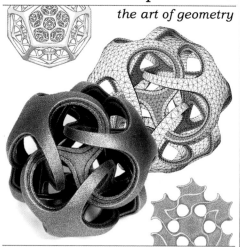

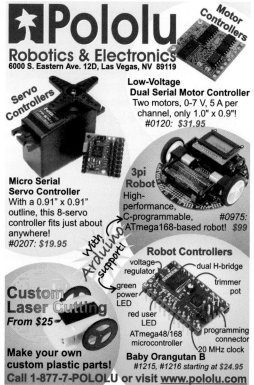

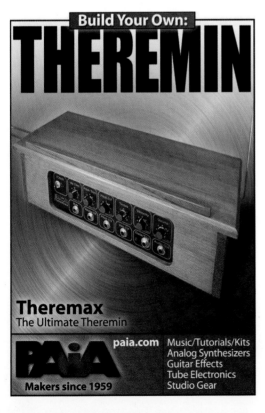

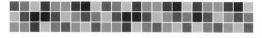

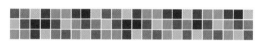

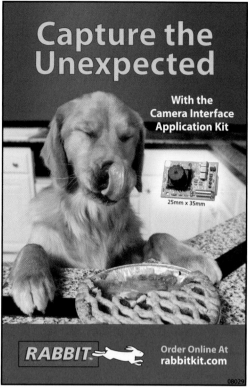

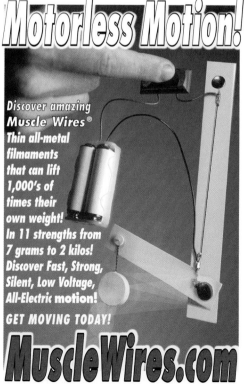

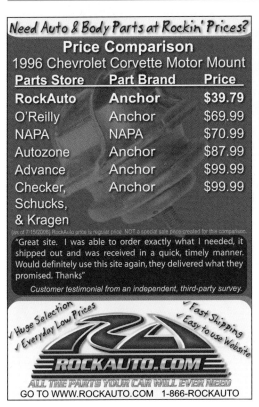

HOMEBREW

My Own Laser Tag System
By Jim Robertson

In 2002, while stationed with the Air Force in Frankfurt, Germany, I started working on a home-built laser tag system. I thought it would be an interesting project and a fun outdoor activity for my kids and their friends (and me).

Commercial outdoor laser tag guns were far too expensive, while consumer toy systems were too fragile and lacked the features I wanted, and neither option was upgradeable or expandable. I was fairly confident I could build something better.

Part of my Air Force training involved use of the MILES (Multiple Integrated Laser Engagement System) during annual field exercises. MILES is like laser tag on steroids, so I incorporated some of its capabilities into my system. I also borrowed ideas and inspiration from first-person shooter computer games my son was playing, like sound effects, automatic respawns, ammo dumps, and health pickups.

The electronics hardware is based on a Microchip PIC microcontroller, and the firmware provides a comprehensive set of parameters that can be edited before each game. As a result, each tagger can be set to inflict various degrees of damage and rates of fire. A backlit LCD display shows your remaining rounds, health, elapsed time, and who tagged you last. A Winbond ISD2560 ChipCorder provides realistic sound effects that can be easily programmed with *.wav* files borrowed from video games, movies, or virtually any source.

The body of the tagger is built mainly from aluminum channel and sheet, which are rugged and easy to work with common hand tools. To keep the system eye-safe, an infrared LED and dual-convex (magnifier) lens are used instead of a real laser. The optics assembly is simply a short PVC tube with the lens at one end and the infrared LED on the other.

I started building MilesTag as a hobby, but it's turned out to be more than that. I've spent more time with my kids, become more active, and even launched a small side business. I continue to improve the MilesTag DIY laser tag system, which is in use by many hobbyists around the world. But I also now design hardware and firmware for one of the largest outdoor laser tag manufacturers in the world.

Jim Robertson is a retired Air Force master sergeant and avid electronics tinkerer. He's an engineering technician at the U.S. Air Force Research Laboratory in Dayton, Ohio.

Photograph by Jim Robertson